FOUL DEEDS & SUSPICIOUS DEATHS IN BOLTON

FOUL DEEDS AND SUSPICIOUS DEATHS Series

Foul Deeds and Suspicious Deaths series explores in detail crimes of passion, brutal murders, grisly deeds and foul misdemeanours. From Victorian street crime, to more modern murder where passion, jealousy, or social depravation brought unexpected violence to those involved. From mysterious death to murder and manslaughter, the books are a fascinating insight into not only those whose lives are forever captured by the suffering they endured, but also into the society that moulded and shaped their lives. Each book takes you on a journey into the darker and unknown side of the area.

Other titles in the series

Please contact us via any of the methods below for more information or a catalogue.
WHARNCLIFFE BOOKS
47 Church Street – Barnsley – South Yorkshire – S70 2AS
Tel: 01226 734555 – 734222 Fax: 01226 724438
E-mail: enquiries@pen-and-sword.co.uk - Website: www.wharncliffebooks.co.uk

Foul Deeds & Suspicious Deaths in
BOLTON

GLYNIS COOPER

Series Editor
Brian Elliott

Wharncliffe Books

First published in Great Britain in 2005 by
Wharncliffe Books
An imprint of
Pen & Sword Books Ltd
47 Church Street
Barnsley
South Yorkshire
S70 2AS

Copyright © Glynis Cooper, 2005

ISBN 1-903425-63-8

Typeset in 11/13pt Plantin by Andy Hemingway, Barnsley.

Printed and bound in England
By CPI UK

Pen & Sword Books Ltd incorporates the Imprints of
Pen & Sword Aviation, Pen & Sword Maritime,
Pen & Sword Military, Wharncliffe Books,
Pen & Sword Select, Pen & Sword Military Classics
and Leo Cooper.

For a complete list of Pen & Sword titles please contact
PEN & SWORD BOOKS LIMITED
47 Church Street,
Barnsley,
South Yorkshire,
S70 2AS,
England
E-mail: enquiries@pen-and-sword.co.uk
Website: www.pen-and-sword.co.uk

Contents

Introduction

This collection of true stories featuring murders and foul deeds in Bolton show one northern mill-town, which also happens to be the home of Bolton Wanderers, in a more disturbing way than the town is usually portrayed. During the nineteenth century in particular it is tempting to think of the place as a 'murderer's Mecca' but that is to kaleidoscope all the cases together. The murder rate seems to have been one or two per year on average; certainly more than today; but it must be seen within the context of the upheavals that Bolton was undergoing as the Industrial Revolution transformed the small pretty country town into a centre for cotton manufacturing and bleaching works, increased its population six fold and more; and generated the worst living conditions in its history. Ordinary life became unbearable for many; drinking their only form of escape. Tempers flared; fights occurred; robberies happened; husbands attacked their wives; children suffered. Bolton was no better and no worse than many other northern industrial towns.

A picture montage of Bolton from a postcard sent in 1917. Author's collection

The book begins with a summary of Bolton's history including its quainter aspects, such as the Bolton elephants and the town's reputation as the 'Geneva of the North', to set the scene and give a context for the stories: this is followed by two brief eyewitness accounts of Bolton in the nineteenth century which is when most of the stories take place. Stories are not grouped chronologically but are arranged to try and give maximum interest. The collection is by no means inclusive of every murder case or foul deed which has taken place in Bolton. It is a cross section spanning four centuries, taking 'man's inhumanity to man' as a common theme, which chronicles death and dishonour in a variety of guises.

Background to Bolton

Bolton Parish covers quite a large area, much of which used to be open moorland. Bolton itself is divided into Great Bolton

Newport Street, showing some of Bolton's 'famous elephants'. The author

and Little Bolton by the River Croal which runs east to west through a deep valley splitting the town. There are over a dozen small 'townships' in the Parish which include: Blackrod, Bradshaw, Breightmet, Darcey Lever, Edgworth, Little Lever, Lostock, Rivington, Sharples, Tonge-with-Haulgh, Turton, and Westhoughton. Within a five mile radius lie Farnworth, Halliwell, Horwich, Stoneclough and Kersley, which are other places of note closely associated with Bolton and the location for some of the stories related in this book.

The name Bolton comes from Old English and simply means an enclosed or fenced dwelling house. However, earlier settlers at Bolton came long before any name was given to the place. On the Turton Tower estate, over looking Egerton, there used to be a near perfect stone circle about fifteen metres in diameter. Sadly in 1871 a tenant farmer smashed up the stones with sledgehammers, presumably for building materials. A second circle lies to the south of it in an equally ruinous condition. The circles date back to the Bronze Age, or even the late Neolithic period, when most of England was part of a huge ritual landscape dedicated to ancient gods and goddesses now lost to history.

As the origin of its name indicates, the first settlement at Bolton took place in Saxon times; a period when the foundations of many towns and villages in modern Britain were laid down. It probably began as just a single farmstead fenced around for protection. The first official mention of Bolton comes in 1067, just after the Conquest, when the Manor of Bolton was recorded as being owned by the Montgomery family. William the Conqueror finally gave the Manor to Ranulf de Bricasard, third Earl of Chester.

In 1251 Henry III granted the town its first Charter to allow a market to be held in Churchgate and an annual fair. By then *Bowelton*, as the Charter quaintly refers to Bolton, was held by William de Ferrers, Earl of Derby. The Earl was to have *the lands and free warren* in the Manor of *Bowelton* and he was granted:

> *permission to hold a market at his aforesaid Manor of Bowelton, in the Country of Lancaster, every seventh day; and*

also at the same place a fair once a year, extending over three days, that is to say on the even and on the day and on the morrow of the feast of St Margaret the Virgin [her feast date falls in the latter half of July].

On 14 January 1253 The Earl of Derby granted his own Charter to Bolton so that it became officially a market town and a borough; and according to *Pigot's Directory* of 1830:

...the lords of the manor hold a court leet annually, in October, at which are appointed a borough reeve, two constables, a deputy constable, and some inferior officers...

The moors around Bolton were ideal for sheep farming and the town was part of the woollen industry of north west England in the Middle Ages. Although the spun woollen yarn was of

The Great Seal of King Henry III, 1270. Brian Elliott

reasonable quality, weaving skills were lacking and woven cloth from north west England had a reputation for being coarse and rather low quality. Edward III (1327-1377) recognised that exports of good woven cloth would be more valuable than simply exporting woollen yarn. Edward had been impressed with the skills of the Flemish weavers when he was away fighting on the Continent. Consequently, he invited a number to settle in England on the understanding that they shared their weaving skills with their English neighbours. This was clearly a successful move since in 1540 John Leland, antiquary of Henry VIII, could write in his itinerary that:

> ...*Bolton upon Moore market stondeth most by cottons* [a type of woollen napped weave] *and course yarne. Divers villages in the moores about Bolton do make cottons...*

He also referred to another Bolton industry:

> ...*they burn at Bolton...se cole* [coal], *of wich the pittes be not far off...*

It was in the 1540s and 1550s that Bolton, which lay in a predominantly Catholic area, acquired a reputation as the 'Geneva of the North.' It has been surmised that this was due to the textile trade and not farming being the dominant industry and that therefore there was much more contact with the more Protestant south and with foreign merchants. This may have been partly true but it also stems from the fact that several active Protestant reformers came from this area. Thomas Lever, from Darcy Lever, one the most passionate and well known reformers was Master of St John's College in Cambridge. His brothers, Ralph and John, were at Cambridge as well, following the teachings of Luther and Calvin. James and Leonard Pilkington from Rivington were also active Protestants and leading debaters. Last but not least there was George Marsh from Bolton, staunchly Protestant and preaching the New Testament, who was prepared to die for his beliefs.

Bolton suffered some turbulent times under the Tudor and Stuart monarchs as the stories of Sir Thomas Pilkington (*The Good Lord of Bolton*), George Marsh (*Martyr at the Stake*) and James Stanley (*The First War Criminal*) in this collection show; and the terrible massacre of Bolton citizens during the Civil War is something that will not be forgotten. However, by 1700, Bolton stood on the threshold of the most defining period in its history when the face of the town changed forever.

There had been a fulling (cloth felting) mill on the banks of Eagley Brook in Bolton as early as 1483 and by the eighteenth century bleaching was a well established cottage industry in the area. It was a lengthy process which involved cloth being left out in the sun to bleach and dry for long periods of time so penalties for theft were severe as in the story of James Holland in *The Hanging on Bolton Moor*. By the end of the eighteenth century the cotton mills had come to Bolton and bleaching became more mechanised. Two of the important inventors of cotton manufacturing machinery lived in Bolton: Samuel

Wood Street, off Bradshawgate, showing former weavers' cottages. The author

Crompton and Richard Arkwright; but as the story of *Hall i' th' Wood* demonstrates the cotton industry made people ruthless and greedy with tragic outcomes. On the other side of the coin the new machinery cost jobs and workers became desperate and finally violent as their livelihoods disappeared as in the story of *A Luddite Tragedy*.

There was industrial unrest throughout the nineteenth century in Bolton due to low wages, high prices, long hours and appalling conditions. Huge profits were made by a comparative few during the boom of the cotton industry at the expense of hundreds of thousands of workers condemned to a life of poverty and toil in the twilight world of the mills. Bolton had been granted Chartered Borough status by Queen Victoria in 1838, incorporating some of the 'townships', which increased the population even more. In August 1839 there were Chartist riots by workers demanding that the

Below: *Whitaker's Emporium (established 1829) dominated Deansgate in the middle of the nineteenth century.* The author
Left: *The soaring spire of Bolton Town Hall.* The author

Above: Some of what remains of the nineteenth century Bolton millscape. The author

Right: Improved Corliss engine, by Hicks & Hargreaves, engineers, Bolton. The author

Government and employers agree to a people's Charter of basic working rights. These riots were followed in 1842 by the 'Plug' riots when rioters drew or pulled the plugs out of factory boilers causing extensive and expensive damage to machinery. Then there was a potato famine and food shortages in 1847 and a cholera outbreak in 1848-49.

The nineteenth century was a wretched time for many Bolton citizens. Dark Satanic chimneys belched their thick smoke over the town while inside the mills men, women and children worked frantically to keep up with the speed and voracious appetite of the machines in a deafening ceaseless roar of noise. The destruction of cottage industries caused population explosions in towns as people came from the land to try and find work in the mills. In Bolton the population multiplied itself six times over within fifty years (from 1783-1821). Many lived in unspeakable and overcrowded conditions in cramped little houses and damp cellars; badly fed and poorly clothed. For most hope had ceased before they were born. Alcohol offered the main form of escape. There were numerous inns and ale houses and drunkenness was rife. Men beat their wives, their children and their dogs. Violence was an everyday occurrence. Murder and foul deeds were common.

The rest of the stories in this collection come from the nineteenth century. People did the most dreadful things to each other with axes, knives, razors, guns, poison, clogs and their bare fists. Men beat, knifed, and strangled their wives and their sweethearts; disposed of their children; kicked their brothers to death; fought their friends. Women poisoned their husbands; drowned their children; sometimes killed other women. It wasn't uncommon for the murderer to commit suicide after killing his victim which happens in the stories *The Axe Murder* and *The Jealousy of Thomas Davies*. The newspapers delighted in long salacious reports of *shocking 'orrible murders and foul deeds*. In many ways it sounds a miserable time to have been alive.

There is not room in this volume to include all the murder cases of the nineteenth century and there is a cut-off point of 1903. This is not because Boltonians suddenly stopped murdering each other or committing foul deeds. They didn't; although the murder rate declined dramatically in the twentieth century. The reason for excluding more recent cases is out of sensitivity because it could cause anguish or distress to friends and relatives of those involved who are still alive.

On a more light-hearted note is the story of Bolton's elephants. There are statues of elephants; sometimes carrying castles on their backs; around Bolton and there are models of baby elephants trotting through the shopping centre. The origin of this delightful, if eccentric, choice of symbol, is obscure. The most likely explanation lies in the colonial links between India and Bolton, occasioned by the dyeing and cotton trades. In India the elephant was a well used method of transport and a castle is a symbol of a howdah which was strapped to the elephant's back to carry goods and passengers.

In 1890 an elephant was incorporated into the former Bolton County Borough coat of arms by Major Ottley Perry. India played a major part in the cotton trade at that time; but Bolton was also said to have military links with India, and elephants are used in war with special military howdahs. One of the first recorded uses of an elephant in Bolton was on the official stamp to the Board of Trustees in 1799. This date would be entirely in keeping with both trading and military links between Bolton and India. During the closing decades of the nineteenth century the symbol of the elephant was used as a watermark on cloth exported from Bolton to signify strength and quality as well as the place where the cloth had been manufactured.

The cast iron 'elephant and castle' in Victoria Square is one of a pair which adorned the gateway of Bolton Bleachworks until 1977. There are models or crests of elephants, mostly with castles, all over Bolton; notably on the Bank of Bolton in Deansgate; over the old schoolrooms in Great Moor Street; at Ashburner Street Market, and on the War Memorial in Victoria Square. When the celebrated traction engine owner and chimney demolisher Fred Dibnah died in Bolton (2004) a model of an elephant was included on his cortège.

Bolton in the Nineteenth Century

The setting for most of the stories of murder and foul deeds in this collection is nineteenth century Bolton and its townships. To give a truer idea of what Bolton in the nineteenth century was really like it is necessary to see it through nineteenth century eyes; so the following are extracts from works of writers of that time, telling of the history, state and growth of their town as they saw it and of the immensely important part that the textile trade, especially cotton, played in its development. These writers, however, are fairly upbeat about the town and do not really portray the suffering or the downside of Bolton, in the way that writers like Friedrich Engels or Mrs Linnaeus Banks wrote about Manchester.

BOLTON, or GREAT BOLTON in 1830

'...Bolton, or Great Bolton, a market town, parish, and township, in the hundred of Salford, 11 miles N.W. from Manchester, and 196 from London. Inhabitants 22,037. Market on Monday. Fairs July 30th and 31st, October 13th and 14th, for horses, horned cattle, and cheese. The petty sessions

Elephant and Howdah, Victoria Square. The author

for the Bolton division, in the hundred of Salford, are held here. The chapelry of Little Bolton to the north is separated by the small river Croal; together they form the large and populous town of Bolton-le-Moors; each of the townships is governed by its own borough reeve and two constables, annually elected. Bolton is situated among the moors, in a soil sufficiently sterile.

The church of Bolton is an ancient edifice, exhibiting nothing remarkable, unless it be the preservation in its windows of the coats of arms of the families of Chetham and Bridgman. A new and handsome church, in the Gothic style, has lately been erected in Bradford Square. All Saints and St. George's Chapels are both in Little Bolton. The places of worship belonging to the Dissenters are numerous, amounting to sixteen; and Bolton abounds in various schools and charitable institutions. The grammar school was founded by the will of Robert Lever in 1641, in which Robert Ainsworth, the eminent lexicographer, received a part of his education.

The principal streets of Bolton, two of which are nearly a mile in length, unite at the market place; the houses, having most of them been erected within the last fifty years, present a very handsome and respectable appearance; and new streets and a square are in daily progress. Here are a theatre, and assembly and concert rooms: a town-hall for the transaction of public business has been recently erected. The market is well supplied with provisions and the town with water and gas...

The canal to Manchester, from which is a branch to Bury, has added materially to the prosperity of the place; and the new railway to Leigh, by affording facilities for an additional supply of coal, has reduced the price of that indispensable fuel. Bolton is noted as one of the earliest stations of the cotton trade in England, if not its original seat. Leland's account of the place is extremely characteristic:

> Bolton upon Moore Market standeth most by cottons and course yarne; divers villages in the moores about Bolton do make cottons...

These cottons, however, were in reality woollens. The vegetable substance, the produce of the cotton shrub, the Gossypium of botanists, not being manufactured in England before the reign of James I., and even till about the year 1773, the fabric called cottons generally consisted of a warp of linen yarn, imported from Ireland or Germany, and shot with a cotton weft; however velvets, counterpanes, and some other articles, were made here as early as 1756, entirely composed of cotton.

Originally fustians were a great branch of the Bolton manufacture, introduced, it is said, by some Protestant refugees soon after the revocation of the Edict of Nantes, 1685; but at present the muslin, dimity, and quilting branches, seem most to prevail. A large proportion of the goods manufactured here are sold to the Manchester merchants, which was not formerly the case, as the dealers from various parts of England came hither to make their purchases.

The spinning mule was invented by Samuel Crompton, a weaver who lived in Hall in the Wood mansion on the outskirts of Bolton. This machine combining the powers of two former inventions, the spinning-jenny and the water frame, was subsequently termed a mule, which name it still retains; and it is in universal use throughout the cotton manufacture.

Sir Richard Arkwright resided in this town in the capacity of a barber about the year 1768, at the period that he had the address (to call it by the softest appellation) to possess himself of a model of the water frame for spinning twist by rollers, just invented by Thomas Highs of Leigh, the original inventor also of the spinning-jenny, and by the appropriation of which to himself, by a patent, he ultimately acquired an immense fortune.

Bolton is distinguished for the extent and excellency of its bleaching concerns. The parish is extensive, abounding in moors, the soil for the most part sterile, but compensated by its hidden wealth, an abundant supply of coal. The following is an enumeration of its townships and chapelries :

	Inhabitants
Anglezarke	215
Blackrod	2436
Bolton, Great	22,037
Bolton, Little	9258

Bradshaw	713
Breightmet	963
Edgworth	1729
Entwistle	677
Harwood	1809
Lever Darcy	956
Lever, Little	1854
Longworth	238
Lostock	576
Quarlton	320
Rivington	583
Sharples	2065
Tong with Haulgh	1678
Turton	2090
Entire population	50,197

Bolton and Bury Canal

Bolton and Bury Canal. This work, for which an act of parliament was obtained in 1791, begins on the west side of Manchester from the river Irwell, to which it runs parallel in a northerly course, crossing it at Clifton by an aqueduct, and again near Little Lever, near which place a branch runs to Bury. Its total length is fifteen miles, with a rise of 157 feet; the country with which this canal opens a communication abounds in coal, together with other mineral products.

Little Bolton

Bolton, Little, a chapelry in the parish of Great Bolton, hundred of Salford, separated from the north of Great Bolton by a small rivulet. Inhabitants 9258. All Saints Chapel, in this township, is about a century old, but presents nothing remarkable. St. Georges is a more recent erection, 1796.

The above sections are reproduced from *The New Lancashire Gazetteer or Topographical Dictionary 1830* with grateful thanks to the website *www.mancuniensis.info/* which covers the historical and genealogical information for the whole of the Salford Hundred.

Bolton and some of its townships (from Pigot's 1830 Lancashire Directory)

...Bolton has arrived at a great point of consequence within the last fifty years, a variety of causes combining to produce such effect; one of which is, its vicinity to Manchester, and the other to the abundant supply of coal with which it is surrounded; and at this period there are in the town and its immediate vicinity, upwards of twenty factories worked by more than thirty steam engines, of the aggregate power of 700 horses; and other factories are in progress of erection upon a large scale. The bleach works, foundries, & machine makers, also employ a great number of steam engines, and it is estimated that the labour performed by steam in the town and direct neighbourhood, would require at least 1,450 horses.

Originally fustian, jeans, thicksetts, and similar fabrics, were the principal articles woven here, but they have been superseded by plain and fancy muslins, calicos, power loom fabrics, quiltings, counterpanes and dimities, which are now the prevailing manufactures. Bleaching is carried on to a great extent: six millions of pieces being the average number bleached annually in the parish.

The advantages of inland navigation, in common with numerous towns in this county, are attached in a valuable degree to Bolton; its canal to Manchester, and a branch to Bury, forming an excellent conveyance for the manufactures of the place as well as for passengers: and a rail-road is making from here to the canal at Leigh, which is expected to be of great advantage in bringing coal to the town.

The public improvements in the town of Bolton have of late years exhibited themselves in a most extensive degree, embracing both utility and ornament. The town is lighted with gas, and plentifully supplied with water: new squares have, within a few years, been formed; and within these four years upwards of six hundred and twenty new houses have been built in Great and Little Bolton.

The public buildings are two handsome town-halls, assembly rooms, theatre; and the recent erections, adding consequence to the town, are the exchange buildings, and a handsome new church, dedicated to the Holy Trinity... the parish church of

St.Peters [is] an ancient structure...All Saints chapel in Little Bolton... St. Georges church, also in Little Bolton...there are besides, episcopal chapels in the parish...the dissenters chapels in Great and Little Bolton are for the various denominations of Methodists, the Unitarians, Swedenborgians, Baptists and Catholics.

The charitable institutions are numerous, and consist of a dispensary; a ladies clothing society, for the necessitous poor; a lying-in charity, &c.: besides which, the free, national, and Sunday schools, nineteen in number, impart instruction to more than 7450 children. Bolton has its mechanics institutes; philosophical and Bible societies...

For the gratification of the student and politician, news and reading rooms are established; and two weekly journals, the Bolton Chronicle and Bolton Express are published on Saturday. The market days are Wednesdays and Saturdays, which are exceedingly well supplied with provisions of all kinds. Fairs are 30th and 31st of July, and 13 and 14th of October, for cattle, horse, pigs, and pedlary; a fortnight fair is also held for lean cattle, on Wednesdays, from 5th of January to the 12th of May.

The progress of population has been very rapid in Bolton; in the 1773 only 5,339 inhabitants were in the two townships; in 1801 Great Bolton contained 12,549, and Little Bolton 4,867; in 1821 Great Bolton contained 22,037 and Little Bolton 9,258 inhabitants. The whole parish contains twelve townships and six chapelries, and in the last named year 50,197 persons.

Turton, a village in Bolton parish, 5 miles north of that town, is situated upon the site of a Roman road...a fair is held here on the 4th & 5th September for cattle.

Darcy Lever, two miles E.S.E. of Bolton, and **Little Lever**, three miles from that town, are two small villages in the parish of Bolton. At the former place is a stupendous aqueduct of three arches over the Irwell; and the neighbourhood abounds with coal. At Little Lever is Lever Hall, an ancient structure, once the residence of Bishop Bridgeman.

Halliwell, a township, in the parish of Dean... two miles W.N.W. of Bolton, in which is Smithills Hall...the great bleaching works of Messrs. Ainsworth & Co. are also here, giving employment to a great number of the inhabitants.

Horwich ... is five miles W.N.W. of Bolton...a new road is nearly finished leading from hence to Bolton, which, when completed, will shorten the distance considerably. The bleaching works of Messrs. Ridgeways at this place are upon a very large scale.

Farnworth is 3 miles S.S.E. of Bolton...at Farnworth mills are the extensive paper works of Messrs. Cromptons, the sole proprietors of the patent paper drying machinery.

Kersley township, situated four miles and a half S.S.E. of Bolton, is dependent upon extensive bleaching works, and the spinning and manufacturing (of) cotton...

For the full transcription of the complete article on Bolton and to research other Lancashire towns in the nineteenth century see *www.genuki.org.uk/big/eng/LAN/Bolton/history.html*

Today, Bolton Metropolitan Borough covers 140 square kilometres (54 square miles). This includes the whole of Bolton and the presently remaining townships of Blackrod, Farnsworth, Horwich, Kersley, Little Lever, South Turton, and Westhoughton.

Market Street, Bolton, in 2004, built on the site of former markets. The author

CHAPTER 1

A Murder and a Suicide
1869

I'll show you who's gaffer

Ellen Allsop was born in 1835, the daughter of Henry Allsop, a weaver, and his wife, Alice, of Fitton House, Lever Street, in Bolton. She worked as a frame tester at Higson and Biggs mill. In 1868, when she was twenty-three, she met and fell in love with Roger Whittle, a 'hooker-on' at the colliery of Elwood Johnson in Swan Lane, about two miles from Westhoughton. The young couple were very much in love and married at St Bartholomew's Church on New Year's Day in 1869. Roger was an industrious young man and he lived in a pleasant detached house in Chapel Walks that had formerly belonged to his grandmother. Ellen had made a good match.

By the time springtime came Ellen knew she was expecting their first baby. Both she and Roger were delighted and looked forward eagerly to the baby's birth. The only cloud on their happiness was Roger's father, Henry Whittle. Since their marriage he had lived with them, but he was not an easy man with whom to share a house because he was subject to fits of uncontrollable temper and, in modern idiom, he had a 'short fuse.' Life was not as harmonious as it might have been for Roger and Ellen.

In July of that year Ellen and Henry had a serious quarrel. Ellen had been mopping the floor but, suddenly realising the lateness of the hour, she stopped to prepare Roger's dinner and had left the cleaning unfinished. For some reason this annoyed Henry intensely. There was a row which ended with Ellen telling Henry that he should find somewhere else to live. Henry was outraged and complained bitterly to his son but, to his fury, Roger supported his wife's decision. Some new houses were being built nearby which belonged to Mrs Ellen Seddon and so Henry reluctantly arranged to rent one of them from her as soon as they were ready.

Henry now became even more bad tempered. He was morose and irritable, and his resentment of Ellen grew and festered. Soon afterwards he arrived home drunk at one in the morning to find the door locked. Roger and Ellen were in bed. Henry hammered away at the door and eventually Roger got up to let him in. There was a huge row and Henry sulked even more about what he saw as his unfair treatment.

By now he was constantly in a bad mood. His sister, Ann Holden, who was married to a hose draper and lived at Derby Street in Bolton, came to visit neighbours. He had a row with her in the street, saying he didn't know what she was doing there and that she always brought mischief with her. He was on bad terms with most of his family and Ann ignored him.

As the time approached when he would leave Roger and Ellen's home, Henry laid claim to several pieces of furniture in the house which he said had belonged to his mother. He repaired a clothes horse (or maiden) so that he could take it with him and this caused another row with his son who believed that the item belonged to him. Roger was so angry that he went to fetch the local constable, PC Hardacre, but the

Derby Street, Bolton, where some of the Whittle family lived. The author

police constable was out. When he returned to the house Henry had quietened down and was upstairs winding bobbins. This was something he had never done before. Ellen and Roger were disturbed by his seemingly strange behaviour and locked their door when they went to bed.

Next morning Roger left for work as usual at four thirty. By seven o'clock Henry was also at his work in the mill shed of T Kemp and Sons, but he returned to the house for breakfast at eight-thirty. While he was there Esther Hall, a friend of his former wife's, came to call. Henry's wife had left him eight years before on account of his violent temper. Esther had come to 'squeeze' (wring and mangle) her washing. Henry told her to get out. Ellen told her to stay, rounding on Henry, telling him that he was only the lodger and she would have whom she liked in the house.

As Whittle was returning to work he saw one of his sisters, Catherine Whittle, who lived with his mother in Wade Lane, pass the house. She was with another of his sisters, Elizabeth Platt, and they were on their way to Thomas Grundy's shop to buy some milk. Ellen, who'd got out her broom and was sweeping in front of the house, asked them in. Henry roared his disapproval. Ellen told them they were welcome, saying that Roger, not Henry, was the 'gaffer' in the house. Henry said he'd show them who was 'gaffer'. He ran into the house, closing the door and shutting Ellen out in the street. Catherine jeered at him and called him a 'pretty man' to which he replied angrily that if she came into his house he'd make her 'pretty'. Catherine shrugged her shoulders and walked away but Henry followed her, sneering at her because he believed that she had sold the old oven and grate from Roger's house to the landlord when they belonged by rights to Henry, or so he thought. Catherine ignored him, like her sister Ann had done, and Henry sulked back to his work.

At lunchtime that day, Ellen's mother, Alice Allsop, called round to see her. Getting no reply she went round to Isabella Whittle's house. Isabella was Henry's mother and from her she learned of the quarrels between Henry and her daughter. Alice returned to the house but the door was still locked. She sent a neighbour's lad to fetch some wire with which she tried to pick the lock but she was unsuccessful. By now Alice was thoroughly uneasy and she returned to the Whittle's house. This time Catherine accompanied her and managed to climb up and peer through the kitchen window where she saw Ellen lying on the floor. She thought she had had a fit but when Alice climbed up and looked in as well she saw how still her daughter's arm was and she knew she was dead. By now a crowd had gathered and someone fetched a ladder. Michael Hodgkinson from the *Grapes Inn* climbed through the window and opened the door, revealing a terrible tragedy.

Upstairs, Henry Whittle lay dead, the pillow on his bed soaked in blood and a huge pool of blood on the floor. Ellen lay downstairs in the back kitchen between two upright posts of an old loom, the treadle of which served as a coal rack, There was a contusion on the back of her head. On the left side a gash made by three wounds extended from the back of the head across the face, cutting through the bone and upper lip and completely dividing her left ear. She too lay in a pool of blood, the axe beside her. She was quite dead and her unborn child had died within her.

Ellen Whittle, horribly mutilated, lies dead in a pool of blood. Hannah Niblett

An inquest was held and a picture of what happened was painfully pieced together. About an hour after Catherine and Elizabeth had left the house Ellen went to Robert Martin's greengrocer's shop to buy a pound of carrots and a cabbage. Henry had gone back to his work but left again at around ten o'clock and was seen hurrying home with his head bent and deep in thought. Judging by the position in which various household items found it seemed that Ellen was in the parlour cleaning a kettle and a fender. They had yet another quarrel, this time about what had happened earlier that morning. Ellen had recently given up work as she was getting very near her time for the baby to be born and she hated Henry and his constant rowing. Resignedly, she had got up and gone to sweep the back kitchen just to get out of his way. Henry followed her and hit her hard on the back of the head with his collier's pick. Ellen slumped to the floor unconscious. Seizing an axe kept on the woodpile kept in the back kitchen he '...completed his terrible work by hewing her in the face...'

Henry had then locked up the house and gone to the nearby butcher's shop managed by John Hilton. He had asked the price of a pound of beef and on being told it was eight pence swore he'd never eat beef again. He seemed very agitated and his hands trembled violently while he constantly mopped his brow. Leaving the astonished butcher staring after him he returned home and went upstairs. He took off his clogs, coat and neckerchief and lay down on his bed. Then he took a razor and cut his throat, hurling the razor across the room after he had done the deed.

The Coroner's jury returned a verdict of wilful murder and suicide. It emerged during the inquest that Henry Whittle, who was aged forty-eight at the time of his death, was a very violent man of bad character who was an inveterate poacher (often forcing his former wife to accompany him on his poaching expeditions) and who drank heavily sometimes. He was disliked by his family and he, for his part, cherished bitter resentment towards them. He had beaten his wife, Ann, mercilessly and left her for dead more than once. Then he had threatened her with a knife and was finally imprisoned in December 1861 for non payment of a £5 fine imposed for this murderous attack on his wife. The magistrate at the court hearing said that one day he would kill someone if he did not learn to curb his temper. After that, and in fear of her life, his wife had finally found the courage to leave him and went to live at Deb Brow in Westhoughton.

After the inquest was over an attempt was made to bury Henry Whittle in secret, at the dead of night. The time chosen was Tuesday night, the night before Ellen's own funeral. However news of this plan somehow leaked out. As the hearse approached the cemetery in Westhoughton at about ten thirty a crowd of three or four hundred people bearing lanterns and torches arrived at the cemetery gates. As the local newspaper reporter of the day put it '...yells, shrieks and exclamations rent the air..' Feelings against Henry Whittle were running so high that the people wanted to kick, tear and denigrate his corpse. It was with great difficulty that the police kept the crowd at bay but at last the coffin was in the earth and the grave was filled in. Slowly people dispersed to their homes but a police guard was maintained by the grave.

By contrast, Ellen's funeral the following afternoon had a procession of forty mourners but two hundred more people, mostly women, turned up at the chapel to pay their last respects to this well liked young woman whose life had been so brutally ended. She was laid to rest in the Dissenters' part of the cemetery at the Bethel Chapel less than a year since she had stood outside St Bartholomew's Church after her wedding and with the promise of a future with the man she loved so much; the man whose father killed her.

28

CHAPTER 2

The Rose Hill Tunnel Mystery
1829

It was a large bundle sewn up in old sacking

The River Croal flows through the centre of Bolton roughly east to west but since the industrialisation and urbanisation of the nineteenth and twentieth centuries, stretches of the river are culverted as it passes through the town centre before turning south behind St Peter's Church. From there it is culverted again before emerging at Springfield at the eastern end of Bridgeman Street in the area known as Rose Hill. Here, one summer's afternoon in June 1829, two young lads were playing by the mouth of the culvert tunnel; daring each other to run in and try to find the huge spiders which were rumoured to hang from the dark roof of the tunnel.

Suddenly, one of the boys yelled out as he tripped over something in the gloom. It was a large bundle sewn up in old sacking. Buried treasure perhaps. Between them they managed to drag it to the mouth of the tunnel. If it were buried treasure it was a queer treasure and it didn't smell very nice. They began to be frightened and decided to go for help. Two men, who worked for Mr Hilton's butcher's shop on Bradshawgate, happened to be passing. Hearing the boys' cries they went down to the tunnel

The River Croal divides Great Bolton and Little Bolton at Rose Hill Tunnel where John Hooper's body was found. The author

Bradshawgate c. 1907 (from an Edwardian Postcard). Author's collection

mouth to investigate. The bundle lay there; its shape ominous and suggestive. One of the men cut the stitching and looked inside. He jumped back quickly and crossed himself. The sacking contained the body of a man in a fairly advanced state of decomposition.

No one knew who he was. Several people came to look at the body; most probably out of morbid curiosity; but no one could identify him. Stories spread that he was a victim of resurrectionists, or body snatchers, grave robbers who stole dead bodies from their graves for scientific research. Some unfortunates were actually murdered by resurrectionists in the bizarre belief that they could be brought back to life again. Perhaps, people whispered, that was what had happened in this case. They guessed he was an unwary traveller who had fallen into the wrong company.

Eventually the corpse was taken to the nearby *Bridgeman's Arms* as it was here, three days later, that an inquest would be held into the death of this unknown man. Before that happened there was a new development. A man came forward to say that he believed the body was that of his late uncle, Major Robinson, killed when he fell from the top of Culcheth Hall. The Major had, however,

The large bundle, sewn up in old sacking, was dragged from Rose Hill Tunnel. Hannah Niblett

been buried at Leigh and considerable doubt was expressed that he would be found this far from home. Consequently, Major Robinson's grave was re-opened and his coffin exhumed; but his body was found to be still in its last resting place and it was quickly re-interred.

The inquest duly took place. The deceased had been a stout muscular man and it was believed that he'd been dead for some eight to ten days. As to how he came to be in the tunnel under the high road at Rose Hill remained a complete mystery and the Coroner's Jury returned a verdict of 'deceased found dead in a tunnel but no evidence to show how he got there.' It was generally believed to be the work of resurrectionists. The body had not been claimed or formally identified and it was ordered that it be buried in the grounds of Holy Trinity Church. No funeral service was to be performed because it was considered that the body, having been disinterred, had already been buried properly once and therefore a second funeral service was unnecessary.

The Reverend Jenkins of Holy Trinity Church in Bolton was not happy about this because he did not believe the body was the work of resurrectionists. He thought the man was probably a murder victim because, when he was found, one knee was bent in rigor mortis, whereas it would have been straightened if the body had been properly buried. However he was forced to abide by the findings of the Coroner's Jury and the unknown man was buried without ceremony in a quiet part of the churchyard.

Nearly two years passed. Then in late July 1831 Reverend Jenkins was

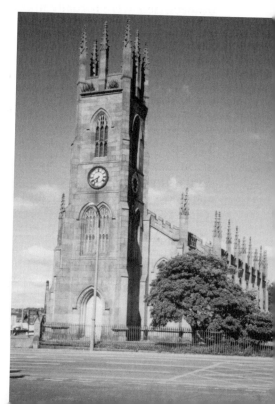

Holy Trinity Church, where John Hooper was buried. The author

contacted by a 'most respectable' lady called Elizabeth Hooper who worked as a housekeeper for a family in Manchester. Her husband, John Hooper, a Bolton saddle maker, had disappeared in the middle of May the previous year, and she had searched for him in vain. Soon afterwards she had moved to Manchester to find work to support herself and her family. While she was in Manchester she began making enquiries.

John Hooper was a master saddler who came from Derby. They had intended to emigrate to America but she had been very close to confinement with her first child. The captain of the ship had refused to take her and her husband had refused to leave without her. So he became a journeyman saddler in the fancy line. He was considered to be first-rate and he was always in work; travelling around a good deal. He had left his family to go to Knutsford on the 15/16 of May in 1829 and disappeared. He was a man of 'sober steady habits', devoted to his wife and children, and she did not believe that he would just leave his family without a word.

The Assistant Travelling Overseer of Manchester had finally taken up her case and began asking around the other journeymen saddlers if they had seen or heard anything of John Hooper. A fellow journeyman saddler named William Brewer said that he knew Hooper and that he had been murdered near Bolton. He then gave further information which he said one of the other journeymen saddlers could corroborate. This sent the Overseer on wild goose chase to the Potteries in search of this second man which Brewer had obviously hoped would forestall any further enquiries.

However, Brewer was also working at a saddlers in Burnley at the time and while there he told them that John Hooper had drowned. When Mrs Hooper heard this she recalled the story of the body in the tunnel at Rose Hill that everyone had been talking about the previous summer. Without further delay she contacted the minister at Holy Trinity Church, saying that she believed that the body found in the tunnel was that of her missing husband, and set off for Bolton to find out for herself what had really happened.

Mrs Hooper gave Reverend Jenkins a detailed description of her husband. He was '...broad set with a prominent forehead, black hair and one of his upper front teeth missing...upon one of his great toes there was a thick clumsy nail...' She added that she had given him a short haircut just before he left home for the last time. The coffin of the unknown man was then exhumed and Mrs Hooper tearfully identified her husband, John Hooper, as the occupant; On Thursday, 28 July 1831 John Hooper was finally buried and given a full funeral service.

In early September Mrs Hooper returned to Bolton to beg the authorities to do all in their power to find her husband's murderer. She told them all she knew and the Assistant Travelling Overseer of Manchester also reported his suspicions. William Brewer had, by then, left Burnley and had worked in both Preston and Liverpool before moving on to Staffordshire. A warrant was issued and Brewer was arrested on 10 September at Burslam in Staffordshire and charged with the murder of John Hooper. On 17 September Brewer was bailed by the Court but he never returned. He simply disappeared into history and nothing more was ever heard of him.

The solving of one mystery created another. Why did William Brewer murder John Hooper? Jealousy or robbery may have been the motive; or perhaps the two men had a violent disagreement. Having 'got away' with his crime for two years, why did Brewer then start to tell conflicting stories which he must have known would cast suspicion on him. Maybe he panicked when he heard that questions were being asked, but it is hard to believe that of a man who carefully sews his victim's body into a sacking shroud and then leaves it in a place where it is unlikely that it will be found, and even if it is, it will be assumed to have been placed there by body snatchers. That shows calm calculated planning to cover up his crime, not the actions of man who will panic if questions are asked. The real mystery of the Rose Hill tunnel murder is that the reasons for its being committed and for the eventual discovery will never be known.

CHAPTER 3

A Shocking Incident
1847

*He was sober enough now and he stared
uncomprehendingly at his dead wife*

Bridget Fitzharris was forty-three and old before her time. She lived at Howell Croft in a house adjoining Kirkman's Foundry with her husband James and her son, Lawrence, or Larry as she affectionately called him, who was twenty-years-old. Lawrence and James were both tailors. At the time of this story they had had a lodger for about five weeks; another tailor named William Wolff who was thirty-two years of age. All of them, except Lawrence, were addicted to drinking, although not alcoholics in the modern sense. The local inn or tavern was a social centre for many people and there wasn't that much other entertainment for people like James and Bridget. Bridget prided herself on having a couple of glasses of ale each night but she couldn't tolerate drink very well. As her own son said, 'we know what she's like after only half a glass.' She seemed to live in a world where people got drunk, slept it off and then simply started again.

On Wednesday, 12 May 1847 James, Bridget and William, or Billy as they called him, were drinking at the *George and Dragon*

Oxford Street, Bolton, today, where Bridget Fitzharris and her companions went drinking. The author

in Oxford Street. Lawrence joined them for a little while at
about five o'clock then left. They had been joined by two other
drinking companions, a couple of young men called Vernon
and Maloney. Around six the five of them went back to the
Fitzharris's house. All were fairly well intoxicated, but when
they arrived at the house Bridget went out and fetched another
jug of beer. They all drank a quart of beer together and then at
seven o'clock James announced he was tired and was going to
bed. Vernon and Maloney left about half an hour afterwards.

At around eight o' clock Bridget popped to see her next door
neighbour, Jane Preston, to ask if she could borrow some
money from Jane's husband, Thomas, a shoemaker. Thomas
was in the yard but Jane said he was out. They didn't have
much money themselves and she didn't want to encourage
Bridget's drinking further. She thought Bridget seemed quite
sober at this point; certainly more so than she had been earlier.
Jane went bed at ten but she was woken a few minutes later by
Bridget calling 'Larry! Larry! My Larry!' She didn't take much
notice however and went back to sleep.

Lawrence returned home at about a quarter to eleven. He
had not seen either of his parents since teatime in the *George
and Dragon*. The door was locked and the key had been taken
from the lock. This puzzled him. Usually if he wasn't home the
door was left unlocked and wedged with a chair. The key was
always left in the lock. He therefore assumed his parents were
still in the *George and Dragon* and retraced his steps to the inn.
Vernon and Maloney were still drinking at the bar and told him
that his parents had gone home hours ago. He went back to the
house and managed to climb in through a side window. It was
very dark. He struck a match but it went out so he groped his
way through to the living room. As he edged his way round he
found his father's waistcoat lying 'where he usually strips
himself' and he could hear loud snoring.

Billy Wolff lay on the floor on his knees and elbows with his
arms resting on Bridget and his head on her head. Bridget lay
flat on her back on the floor. She wasn't stirring and her hand
felt icy to Lawrence's tentative touch. He dragged Billy Wolff
off his mother and got him onto a chair. This woke Billy. He
was still very drunk. Lawrence chafed his mother's hands

calling out 'Mother! Mother!' There was no response.

He saw that the key to the door lay on a chair. Quickly Lawrence unlocked the front door and fetched one of his neighbours, Biddy Brady, and another young woman who was with her. They brought a candle with them which he lit and stood on a saucer. Kneeling down by his mother, he lifted her up into his arms and called her name again and again. 'Mother! Mother!' The noise woke his father who was still upstairs and he called out irritably 'What's to do?' Lawrence stifled a sob. 'Mother's dead!' James padded down the stairs when he heard that. He was sober enough now and he stared uncomprehendingly at his dead wife. Billy was staring glassily at James and Lawrence then he heaved himself off the chair and went upstairs without giving any explanation of what had happened.

Lawrence noticed finger marks on Bridget's throat and a small wound on the left side of her forehead. He laid her carefully on a board and James gave her some warm water although what he hoped to achieve by that isn't clear. At one thirty in the morning Billy, still fully dressed, came down the stairs. Although well accustomed to drink he must have taken a lot, thought Lawrence, for he was still very drunk. It would be no use to ask him anything until he was sober. By six that morning Billy was evidently capable of more coherent thought for he turned to Lawrence and said that it was as well James hadn't fallen out with Bridget or 'clouted' her else he would be under suspicion of killing her.

A few minutes later Jane Preston arrived. She saw the 'blood mark' on Bridget's forehead. Bridget had a black silk handkerchief tied under her chin and when Jane took it off she saw fingernail marks on the Bridget's throat. Jane turned to Billy and said she'd heard shouting at about ten o'clock the previous night. Billy said it must have been James and Lawrence who were arguing; but Lawrence hadn't been home by ten o'clock. At that point James and Lawrence called the police and Billy, still drunk, was arrested.

It seemed strange that the police had not been called before. Lawrence was a devoted son and was deeply upset by his mother's death. Yet though she had obviously been injured he

Bridget lay on the floor. She was not stirring and her hand felt icy. Hannah Niblett

appeared to be very reticent in the way he reacted to Billy Wolff whom he must have suspected of being her attacker since the door was locked from the inside and the key lay on a chair. Both father and son watched Billy go upstairs without a word of explanation but neither of them attempted to demand one.

The inquest was held the next afternoon (Thursday) at the Borough Courtroom with the Coroner and a jury of sixteen local traders and craftsmen. Joseph Denham, the surgeon, confirmed that Bridget had finger nail marks on her throat and bruises on the left side of her forehead and on the underside of her right jaw. Her body was emaciated and there were signs of heart disease. However, the surgeon thought she'd died of either strangulation or suffocation; probably slight strangulation followed by suffocation, considering the symptoms displayed which included losing control of her bodily functions.

Lawrence told the jury that there was no evidence of an affair between Bridget and Billy although he knew his father was frequently tipsy and could have missed the signs. Besides, he said, Billy had his own bed. This was important since it was not unusual for landlords to share their beds with lodgers. After the inquest however, certain facts did come to light which indicated that there might have been 'improper conduct' by Billy towards Bridget. Perhaps he tried to force himself on her (locking the door first in case Lawrence should return home unexpectedly) and she cried out; there was a struggle and in trying to quieten her he hit her and grabbed her by the throat before passing out, crushing her and suffocating her in the process.

The Coroner's jury found Billy Wolff guilty of manslaughter by a majority of twelve to four and he was sent for trial to Liverpool Assizes. However, he was later acquitted and discharged by the Court. In view of the evidence of some sort of struggle, shown by the marks on the body, and the cries, which were never explained, this seems a strange verdict, but no one saw him kill Bridget and, as forensic science still lay in the future, no one could prove he had killed her or harmed her in any way.

CHAPTER 4

A Tragic Cameo
1856

*...bundled up in a man's shirt and left on the
steps of the tavern*

In the *Bolton Chronicle* of 23 August 1856 there was an anonymous snippet of news which would have raised a smile were it not for the waste of a young life which lay behind it. It was reported that a newborn baby girl had been found on the steps of the *Stork Tavern* on Old Hall Street. Just like the traditional image of a stork bringing a new little bundle to begin life on earth, this little girl was wrapped up and left there to begin the story of her life. Tragically, it was a very short story and it did not have a happy ending.

Despite the fact that the baby was less than an hour old when she was found, and although it was summer and she had been wrapped up, her body was very cold and she had already begun to turn blue. The woman who found her gave her a warm bath and wrapped her up in shawls but it was too late. The child died a few hours later. Medical opinion was that she was very weak because she had not been fed and because she was half starved she died of exposure even though she was not naked when she was found. Someone had wrapped a strip around the umbilical cord where it had been cut and the child was dressed in a tiny shirt and skirt and wore a little cap on her head. She had then been bundled up in a man's shirt and left on the steps of the tavern. The baby girl had been too weak to cry much but given the loving care that should have been her due she might have survived.

The mother was said to be Nancy Green, a nineteen-year-old local girl of 'ill repute'. It was doubtful that she would have known who the father was. She had made no effort to try and provide for her child; she did not even have any clothes in which to dress the baby when it was born. Maybe she had never had any intention of trying to provide for her child. It was rumoured that she had given birth on the floor of the pub cellar, on the cold flagstones down there, in the darkness and dampness of the old building. One or two local women helped her in her labour and found some scraps in which to dress the baby. Nancy was not interested in her daughter. After the birth she cleaned herself roughly and then went round to the house of her latest boyfriend leaving others to deal with the problem of the baby.

Nancy was finally arrested and charged but she was quite unconcerned about the whole matter. A doctor examined her and said that she had given birth recently. Nancy did not deny this but she said that no one could prove that the child found on the steps of the *Stork Tavern* was hers. In December of that year she was sent for trial at Liverpool Assizes although she was found not guilty because the legal profession were forced to reluctantly agree with her that they could not prove that the dead baby had belonged to her. Rumours and circumstantial evidence did not amount to proof. Whatever the truth, it was never told and the anonymous little baby girl became just another sad statistic.

Right: *Old Hall Street, where Henry Culshaw lived, and where* The Stork *public house once stood.* The author

Below: *Bolton Town Hall, taken from Oxford Street, c.1903. Old Hall Street is on the right of the photograph.* Author's collection.

CHAPTER 5

A Doomed Romance
1877

George was led weeping from the dock...

George Pigott led a complicated life for a man of just twenty-nine-years-old. He had formerly been employed as a coachman before getting a job as a horse-tram driver. By the end of 1877 however, he was working at the coal mines in Kersley just outside Bolton. He was married with several children but he also had a mistress. Not that he really thought of her like that. He had decided that she was his soul mate and he was obsessed with her. He wanted to live with her and to spend the rest of his life with her, but in 1877 divorce for a man of his station in life was not really an option, so he did the next best thing and persuaded her to run away with him to begin a new life.

Florence Galloway was in domestic service. She had known George Pigott since she was a child. Florence knew that George was married and she knew that what she was doing was wrong but she listened to her heart and not to her head. Eventually he persuaded her to give up her job and her family and live with him as man and wife. He left his wife and children and his job as a horse tram driver and they moved to Birmingham and settled down there in a small cottage.

Their happiness did not last long. Florence began to complain of his 'ill usage' of her and she wanted to leave him. At first that proved impossible because she had no money of her own but she finally returned to her mother on 5 November 1877.

George reluctantly returned to his wife and family. Although he lived with his wife he remained extremely anxious to get Florence back living with him again.

He 'lurked about' outside Mrs Galloway's house. He wrote warm and loving letters to Florence. He said his wife was guilty of her own misconduct so he was no longer either required or needed to support her and therefore he was free to live with Florence again. Mrs Galloway was adamant that Florence should have nothing whatsoever to do with him and this time Florence listened to her head and not to her heart.

On 24 November that year George met Mrs Galloway in a shop and tried yet again to talk to her about Florence and to request permission to see her daughter. Mrs Galloway would have none of it and told him so in no uncertain terms. She forbade him to go anywhere near their house and she told him to leave Florence alone.

George was now becoming desperate so he devised a plan. On 5 December he wrote a letter to Mrs Galloway which purported to come from an old friend of hers, Mrs Wilson, offering both Mrs Galloway and Florence the chance of some work and arranging for the two women to go to her house that evening. He gave it to a small boy to deliver, and then he waited, biding his time and rehearsing what he would say.

Mrs Galloway and her daughter duly set off that evening for Mrs Wilson's house. George, who had been watching and waiting, then appeared in front of them on the path. Mrs Galloway was furious. She realised she had been duped and told George he was 'a bad man.' George said he just wanted to reason with her and her daughter but Mrs Galloway was having none of it. She spoke for Florence, she said, when she told him that he was not wanted and that he should go away and leave them alone.

George tried one last time. 'Are you saying that you will not let me help you in any way, at any time, under any circumstances?' he asked.

'Correct!' snapped Mrs Galloway. 'I refuse to allow you to have any contact whatsoever with my daughter!'

'So be it!' said George and before anyone could stop him he took a pistol from his pocket and shot Florence once in the head.

Florence Galloway died shortly afterwards and George Pigott was arrested at the Kersley coal mine while he was working. He was sent to the Assizes for trial charged with wilful murder but George Pigott was not going to give up easily and hired a very canny defence lawyer. The trial began in mid March 1878.

First, the defence counsel protested, no adequate motive had been established for him shooting Florence. He loved the girl to distraction. She had been shot accidentally when the pistol he'd intended to use to kill himself had discharged itself without warning. A medical witness was produced to testify that in 1869 George had been run over by a 'lurry' and had received head injuries which had changed his personality and left him with suicidal tendencies. This was confirmed by his mother, father and brother. He had in fact intended to kill himself if Florence had rejected him again.

The jury were not convinced. They took just thirty minutes to find him guilty of wilful murder. The Judge gave a censorious little speech about those who 'pass from sin to crime' and then kill those who will not 'submit to their wicked will' before he donned his black cap and pronounced sentence of death on George Pigott. George was led weeping from the dock which rather destroyed his own defence. If he could not live without Florence and really had intended to kill himself and not her, then surely he would have welcomed the prospect of being, so soon, reunited with her in death.

CHAPTER 6

A Portent
1650

...strange phenomena appeared in the skies...

In 1651 the Earl of Derby became the first person to be executed for a war crime: a massacre of the citizens of Bolton in 1644. There was still religious unrest in parts of the country and many secretly believed that the king should not have been killed; but Oliver Cromwell held

James (7th) Earl of Derby, Charlotte, his wife, and Lady Katherine Stanley. their (third) daughter. From a Vandyke painting. Lancashire Record Office

the reins of government with a firm hand and few dared to oppose him. The year before the Earl's execution, and just a few months after the end of the Civil War, strange phenomena appeared in the skies over Bolton.* Some thought them to be signs from God, angry at the defilement of His churches and the murder of the king; others thought 'them wondrous and of unearthly origin; a portent of disasters to come.' One Bolton man, Ellis Bradshaw, tried to be scientific in the description of what he had witnessed when he wrote to a friend in London. Below is a transcription of part of Ellis Bradshaw's letter; hence the quaint English and the idiosyncratic spelling and grammar. The description constituted about a quarter of the letter; the rest being of religious content, since Mr Bradshaw clearly believed that these phenomena were sent by God to draw attention to wrong doings by enemies of the Reformation:

The thing was thus. Yesterday being Monday, February 25th, 1650, being our Market day at Bolton in the Mores in the County of Lancaster, betwixt ten and twelve of the clock, and much of that time there appeared to us all, yea to all in the Town, or in the way thither, that look to high, A white Circle compassing directly from the glorious sun shining in his strength, (the Skie being clear, and not overspread with clouds or mist, &c.) straight into the North, as it were of a levell height, with the height of the Sun, compassing round the Sun again, as if it had been a wall, and the Sun a Postern in the Side of it. And besides the true Sun, there appeared also a great way distant on either side of the Sun, a bright place in the aforesaid Circle, not unlike in greatness to the true Sun, but not so bright nor formable, but rather red and changeable, especially at its vanishing; like part of a bright Rain-bow, or as we call them, Weather-Galls, though far brighter, and more clear and splendrous to all beholders when they were at brightest. There appeared also, in the Northern part of the same Circle, two other likewise, which like bright places of the same colour, but not so bright and splendrous: All which four were set directly in the white Circle, like so many Postern Towers in the walls of a City, a great way distant from each other.

There appeared likewise directly over out heads, two fair

Rain-bows in the clear Skie, the one tending with either end of it, towards the bright places, that were next to the Sun, though they did not reach them. And the other tending with both its ends, as directly pointing at the other two places, that were in the Northern part of the white Circle, that shined also as hath been said: So that these two Rain-bows, that were directly over our heads, with their backs together, and their ends directly one from the other; the one Southwards, and the other Northwards; the one as inclining to embrace the Sun, the other to embrace the North Pole.

All these visible Apparitions continued a great while, some say two hours, but of the certain time I am not certain, for I saw them not at first: but I saw them vanish by degrees away, beginning in the North; for the North-side of the white Circle began to vanish first, and then the two bright places in the North of the Circle did also first vanish before the other, and so also did the North Rain-bow, and then by degrees the other also, so that the nearer to the Sun, was the longer visible, not only of the Rain-bows, but of the bright places, and of the white Circle…

…And therefore, it is observable, that these two Rain-bows were not set in the Skie directly upwards in the usuall manner arch-wise, but they were both in appearance to us as laid aside, like two fallen arches, and that with their backs together, so that their four ends were at the furthest distance from the others that they could possible be…

*Editor's note: This could refer to a rare cloud formation termed 'nacreous cloud' ('nacre' = mother of pearl). It was witnessed in parts of South Yorkshire and Derbyshire on 16 February 1996, described by the BBC *Look North* weatherman as a 'once in a lifetime' phenomenon.

CHAPTER 7

The First War Criminal
1644

He deliberately killed over one thousand people...

War crimes are generally supposed to be a modern concept; an evolution of a social conscience which no longer accepts that the end justifies the means; so it comes as a shock to discover that the first war crimes trial on record in England dates back to the Civil War (1640-1649), centuries before the Geneva Convention which is supposed to govern the conduct of warfare today.

James Stanley, seventh Earl of Derby, was born to a privileged life. He didn't expect it to end in public execution for the crime of 'wilful murder'. However he didn't just murder one person, or even two. He deliberately killed over one thousand people, not in battle, but in a cold blooded revengeful massacre

Right: *The Earl of Derby, awaiting his execution.*

Below: *An engraving depicting the execution of the Earl of Derby at Bolton in 1651.* Lancashire Record Office

which would leave its mark on the Lancashire town of Bolton forever.

He was born in 1607, the son of William Stanley, sixth Earl of Derby, and Elizabeth de Vere. In 1625 James entered Parliament as the Member for Liverpool but by 1628 he had left the Commons and become a member of the House of Lords as Baron Strange. He married Charlotte de la Trémouille, the daughter of the Duc de Thouars, and settled at Lathom House near Bolton. They had a son, Charles, born in 1628, who became the eighth earl after James's execution. His father died in September 1642 and James succeeded to the Earldom. He was a staunch supporter of the Royalist cause in the Civil War. In 1643, the third year of the Civil War, he moved to the Isle of Man and established it as a Royalist stronghold.

While James was in the Isle of Man the Civil War raged on the mainland and his French wife was left to defend Lathom Hall as best she could. By all accounts, Charlotte de la Trémouille, the Countess of Derby, was a formidable lady.

The town of Bolton had only been fortified by an earthen bank. The majority of Boltonians were strongly sympathetic to the Puritan cause and made their allegiance to Oliver Cromwell clear. The town was attacked twice by the Royalists in 1643, on 18 February and 28 March. Each time the Royalists suffered heavy losses and Bolton emerged victorious.

The chair at which James, the Earl of Derby, knelt in prayer when on the scaffold. Lancashire Record Office

By 1644 Lathom House was pretty much alone in holding out for the Royalist cause in the Bolton area. In March 1644 the House was attacked by Parliamentary forces and laid under siege for two months. The besiegers included several Bolton men. Countess Charlotte commanded her household and her defenders astutely. She would not surrender and she fought like a tiger. The inmates of Lathom House were, however, heavily outnumbered until the 28 May when Prince Rupert, the nephew of King Charles I, arrived unexpectedly with an army of twelve thousand soldiers.

The besiegers decided that a tactical retreat would be both advisable and practical and fled to Bolton with Prince Rupert hot on their heels. The town resisted his first attack, but the second attack, led by the Earl of Derby who had returned from the Isle of Man, breached the earthen defences. What followed was a war crime of hideous proportions; although there are two versions of what happened. The first, and most likely, is chillingly described as follows:

...nothing was heard but kill dead, kill dead...killing all before them without by their horsemen pursuing the poor amazed people, killing, spoiling and stripping all they could meet with...denying quarter to any till the sword, drunk with blood, was sheathed...

Bolton, the 'Geneva of the North', a 'sweet Godly place', had turned into 'a nest of owls and a den of dragons.'

In all over one thousand people were massacred and scores more were injured. It amounted to a decimation of the small Lancashire textile town. The second version of this tale tells how the Earl, newly returned from the Isle of Man, and horrified at the siege of his home and of his wife, had ridden to Bolton in a white hot fury and joined the Royalist forces to lead a successful attack on the town. The Roundhead commander, Colonel Rigby, fled with the remnants of his forces, leaving the citizens of Bolton vulnerable to the wrath of the Earl. According to legend the Earl then lined up one thousand Bolton citizens and personally ran them through with his own sword.

The massacre had left the town '...bleeding, dying and undone...' It was certainly bad publicity for the Royalist cause. Though most of the massacre was probably down to Prince Rupert and his men venting their frustrations, it was the Earl of Derby who was held to account in the eyes of the Puritans. In July 1644, following the Royalist defeat at the Battle of Marston Moor, the Earl returned to the Isle of Man. After securing the Island he came back to the mainland and was involved in a number of skirmishes with the Parliamentarian forces until he was finally captured at the decisive Battle of Worcester which took place on 3 September 1651.

Oliver Cromwell was now firmly in charge of the country and was not inclined to be merciful to the likes of the Earl of Derby. The dreadful slaughter at Bolton had not been forgotten and Cromwell was determined that James Stanley should pay the full penalty of the law. The Earl was not allowed a civil trial. Instead he was court martialled and sentenced to death. Cromwell felt it would be appropriate for the sentence to be carried out in Bolton, the town that had suffered so much at the Earl's hands. Accordingly, the Earl was sent back to Bolton under a military escort to be beheaded, and a scaffold was erected at Market Cross on Churchgate opposite the *Swan Hotel*.

He spent his last few hours, mostly in prayer, in a room at the *Man and Scythe*, an ancient hostelry built in 1251 on what is now Deansgate. The inn is still there, although the present

The Man and Scythe *public house where James Stanley, the 7th Earl of Derby, spent his final hours.* The author

building dates from 1636 when it was rebuilt. Lord Clarendon subsequently summed up the Earl's character thus:

> ...*he was a man of great honour and clear courage, and all his defects and misfortunes proceeded from his having lived so little among his equals that he knew not how to treat his inferiors...*

James Stanley maintained his dignity and composure to the end. As he stood on the scaffold before executioner Whowell he said to the assembled crowds:

> *The Lord bless you. The Son of God bless you all of this town of Bolton, Manchester, and especially Lancashire, and God send that you have a King again, and Laws. I die like a Christian, a Soldier, and Christ's Soldier.*

Whowell swung the axe and the Earl paid the supreme penalty. It seemed as if he and Bolton were destined to be each other's nemesis.

Former site of the gallows at the Market Cross in Deansgate where the Earl of Derby was executed. The author

The axe used to execute the Earl of Derby became known as the Derby Axe. It lay hidden for over a hundred years at Whowell's farm on Edgeworth Moor near Turton. In the late 1750s the axe, said to be still bloodstained, was put in a sack with other old iron implements to be auctioned as a job lot. They were sold to James Holt, clerk and sexton of Turton Chapel. The axe remained in the Holt family until 1851 when it was bought by William Sharples of the *Star Inn* at Bolton which stood just yards from where the scaffold had stood on which the Earl was executed on 15 October 1651.

Sharples exhibited the Derby Axe in a museum attached to the *Star Inn*, but both buildings burned down in 1852. The Derby Axe was saved but it was given a new oak haft made from the former altar rail at Turton Old Chapel and the blade was reburnished. Although this restoration was done with the best of intentions it destroyed some of the history and the bloodstains from the unfortunate Earl can no longer be seen.

Deansgate, with St Peter's church and Market cross, where the Earl of Derby was executed in 1651. The author

CHAPTER 8

A Loose Cannon
1866

He told them to go away and stop making a noise...

Guy Fawkes Night 1866 and three lads were celebrating in the time honoured tradition of making as much noise as possible and annoying as many people as possible. John Thompson, aged sixteen, the son of Jonah Thompson, a builder of Bolton, and his friends, George and Samuel Briggs, all lived in Scowcroft Court off Orlando Street in Bolton. Samuel was also sixteen-years-old. They had managed obtain a small old cannon, 'a piece of round drilled iron, to fire on Bonfire Night.

John and George met up about six o'clock on 5 November and had gone to the mill in Vernon Street being built by Mr Thompson. They fired the cannon several times and then they

Orlando Street amd the mill, close to where John Thompson lived. The author

The Cattle Market *public house stands on the site of the inn of the same name, in Orlando Street, close to John Thompson's home.* The author

ended their evening by taking the cannon to some vacant ground behind the house of William Hardman, of Hardman and Hampson manufacturers on Manchester Road at around nine-thirty. Having fired the cannon two or three more times they then decided it was time to leave. Samuel Briggs had heard the noise of the cannon being fired and joined them about twenty to ten.

They were on their way home and passing the back yard door of Mr Hardman's when Mr Hardman's son, John, and his niece, Mary Hardman, came out. John Hardman Junior was twenty-one and a moulder. He told them to go away and stop making a noise because his father was ill. John Thompson looked at him and said insolently 'I am not going to run...'

John Hardman drew himself up, looking angry. 'Are you going to use your lip then?' he asked Thompson sarcastically. Samuel Briggs snorted a laugh, and as he turned away to start for home, John Hardman kicked him. He was not hurt, more surprised. Then Hardman aimed a punch at John Thompson, although he did not succeed in hitting him, and in frustration he kicked him on the legs.

The boys began to run away but Thompson turned and threw the cannon he'd been firing with as much force as he could muster at Hardman. The cannon, weighing just under one kilo, struck Hardman on the left temple and he fell to the ground unconscious. All three then turned and ran away, leaving the cannon on the ground behind them. Mary Hardman gave chase and she caught Samuel Briggs and brought him back. By this time Councillor Best and Joe Sutcliffe, who lived opposite the Hardmans, had carried John Hardman in to the family's kitchen and called for surgeon Roger Hampson to attend.

Unfortunately however, John Hardman never recovered consciousness and he died at five o'clock the following afternoon. John Thompson had been arrested in his bed the previous night and remanded in custody for two weeks. Mrs Thompson was ill in bed at the time and when told what her son had done she became quite delirious. The inquest was held two days later on Thursday afternoon at the Borough Court on Bowkers Brow in Bolton.

A post-mortem examination had been carried out by Dr Carruthers of Churchgate Street and Dr Macintosh in the presence of Alderman Ferguson who watched on behalf of John Thompson. John Hardman had died from compression of the brain resulting from a six inch long fracture of the skull. The cannon had been thrown in overhand style with some force.

John Thompson, George and Samuel Briggs, and Mary Hardman all gave evidence at the inquest. They each gave their own version of what had happened that fateful night. The Coroner pointed out that firing of the cannon was illegal in itself. Mary Hardman had kept the cannon afterwards and given it to her cousin James Hardman. John Thompson was found guilty of manslaughter and committed for trial at Manchester Assizes.

In the event the case never came to Court. The Judge and other learned legal advisers met before the hearing and decided that had been no premeditation or malice aforethought. They regarded the whole episode as an 'accident without anger' and that there was no case to answer. The worst the boys had been guilty of was causing a public annoyance and actually firing the cannon, but then it had been Guy Fawkes Night. John Thompson was acquitted of any crime and discharged.

CHAPTER 9

I Want Further Discourse with You
1858

There were two to three thousand spectators at the funeral...

Old Hall Street in Bolton today is very different from the Old Hall Street of this story. It has been curtailed and half its present length on one side is taken up with the mock Tudor style building which houses Whitakers textile emporium, established in 1879. In 1858 Old Hall Street was a longer street of workers cottages, shops and the *Three Arrows* public house; a cobbled street leading through the centre of the town. It is now a pedestrianised area with modern paving which leads to Victoria Square and the Town Hall.

On a warm June night in 1858 Henry Culshaw, a twenty-eight-year-old engineering fitter at a local foundry, was making his way home to Old Hall Street after a good Saturday night out with friends. He was in fine form, but not being a heavy drinker, he was not singing or carousing or making any other disturbance. On the corner of the Market Square he met an old friend of his, William Duckworth. The pair chatted for a few minutes before William said that he would walk with Henry back to Old Hall Street as it was on his way home.

As they neared Henry's home, which he shared with his widowed mother, Martha Culshaw, they saw three men standing opposite the *Three Arrows* pub. The men were of Irish descent and had obviously enjoyed an extremely convivial night. They were singing and shouting, and, as it turned out, spoiling for a fight. It was by now half past midnight and, as they passed, Henry asked the men to be quiet and stop causing a disturbance and to go home. They turned and stared at him. Eventually the tallest one, who was just in his shirt sleeves owing to the warmth of the night, said to Henry 'I want more discourse with you ...'
'Well I don't!' interrupted Henry. 'Just quieten down.'   He

began to walk off.

The Irishman followed him and tapped his arm.

'I said I wanted more discourse with you.'

'What about?' asked Henry wearily.

'Do you want to fight?' The Irishman looked challengingly at him.

'No.'

William and Henry resumed their walk home. The next moment a punch sent Duckworth flying. What happened to Henry is best told in his own words:

> *The same person* [the tallest Irishman] *then kicked me over the leg and I fell to the ground. The same person that kicked me, and his two companions then rushed on top of me. I screamed out and Mrs Lomax came and pulled the same person off me that had kicked me over the leg. I have seen him often before, though I did not know his name. I can tell him when I see him again...*

Henry would never have the chance to see him again. A few hours later, on Sunday morning at eight o'clock, Henry Culshaw was given medical treatment for a fracture of the right leg and compound dislocation of the right ankle joint. By Monday evening, however, 'mortification' (gangrene) had set in and he was taken to Bolton Infirmary. By Wednesday it was obvious that he was not going to recover so Mr Arrowsmith, one of the Borough magistrates, took a deposition from him as to the events which had led to this unfortunate state of affairs. Henry Culshaw died at four-forty the next morning, Thursday, 24 June 1858.

The inquest was held that same afternoon in Bowker Street. The jury viewed the body and found it very discoloured. Henry Culshaw had been a well liked and well respected young man in the town and a crowd had gathered in Bowker Street. Feeling was running high in the crowd about this murder. There had been much trouble with drunks, especially Irish drunks, causing disturbances and complaints that there were insufficient police officers on the streets to control the Irish. A local Roman Catholic priest condemned the 'low Irish'. William Charnley, of 50 Old Hall Street, and another witness of the fight, also complained about the way the Irish behaved generally and of their readiness for a fight.

Henry Culshaw was buried on Sunday, 27 June in the afternoon at the Cemetery at Tonge. There were some two to three thousand spectators at the funeral and around two to three hundred mourners which included at least two hundred members of the Amalgamated Society of Engineers, Machinists & Co to which Henry had belonged. The crowd was very orderly but there was a large police presence. The cortège started from the *Fleece Inn* on Bradshawgate and wound its way to Culshaw's house on Old Hall Street and then to the Cemetery. Thirty to forty members of the Society of Steam Engine Makers walked from their Clubroom to the

The former Fleece Inn, *on Bradshawgate, where inquests were held and from which Henry Culshaw's cortège left.* The author

Bradshawgate, Bolton, today. The author

Fleece and joined the procession. They stood by the graveside as the coffin was lowered into the grave and then threw pieces of boxwood on top of the coffin following an ancient custom.

The culprits had been speedily apprehended; especially as the Mrs Lomax who had pulled one of them off Culshaw was the wife of the local policeman. They were arrested on 22 June, before Henry Culshaw died, and remanded for two weeks. By the time they appeared before the magistrates they were looking very dejected. Edward Barry, aged forty-four, and Peter Barratt, aged thirty-five, were both Irish shoemakers living in Howell Croft. Naturally they protested their innocence although their case wasn't helped by Barratt's cap being discovered at the scene of the crime or the fact that witnesses could identify them.

Nancy Lomax was the wife of Police Constable Lomax and she lived at the lock-ups in Old Hall Street. She said that at about one or one-thirty on the Sunday morning she had heard noise and arguing in the street. She unlocked the door and saw Henry Culshaw with four or five other men. Henry was complaining about the noise the others were making and he told them to go home. This started the fight. They were on the opposite side of the street, about twenty yards away and opposite the *Three Arrows* entry. Duckworth was struck first; then Henry Culshaw was kicked by all of them. Edward Barry was 'down on Culshaw' while the others gave him a kicking. She ran up and, taking hold of his hair and neckerchief, she pulled Edward Barry off Henry Culshaw. She recognised Barry and she also recognised Peter Barratt, but she did not know the others. When she called for police assistance they all ran off 'up the Three Arrows entry.'

Nancy Lomax and William Duckworth had given chase and Duckworth caught Edward Barry. Duckworth was marching him towards the lock-ups when two women who had been following them attacked Duckworth and 'rescued' Barry. Duckworth had tracked them to where the women lived but the women had 'gone for him' with a poker. Henry meanwhile had managed to drag himself up against the old fire engine house door and said that they had 'purred' his ankle. Richard Aspinall, a moulder who also lived in Old Hall Street, had then carried Henry the forty or fifty yards to the Culshaw home where his shocked mother attended to his injuries. The following morning she had called for medical help.

Edward Barry and Peter Barratt were sent for trial on a charge of manslaughter but before they came to trial a third Irishman named John Kelly was arrested on Thursday 15 July. He was brought before the magistrates as having been involved in the Culshaw incident. Kelly was shoemaker who lived in King Street and he was charged with being 'a principal in the attack.' He had been identified by a witness who went under three different names: John Caman, John Carman and John Cameron. The Public Prosecutor decided to use just one: John Caman. Caman said he had known Kelly for eighteen to twenty years and Kelly had worked for him at times. On the night in question, according to Caman, he witnessed the fight and he said that he had heard John Kelly call out 'Sing into 'em! Sing into em!' and 'em ought to be killed!' as they kicked Culshaw mercilessly. Caman had been standing ten or twelve yards away near the *Three Arrows* and couldn't accurately determine who had administered each kick. However, his evidence was called into question when it was discovered that two years previously he had quarrelled violently with John Kelly and he'd charged Kelly with assault. Kelly had been acquitted.

John Kelly's daughter, Mary, was next called to the witness stand. She said that he came home between ten and eleven o'clock and minded the baby until he went to bed sometime between twelve and one. She had washed his shirt for him. Her mother had been out and came in drunk after her father. John

Kelly and his wife quarrelled frequently about her drinking and he often beat her. The Kelly family lived in a room in the house of Mr and Mrs Edwin Murphy; and they, probably judging by the noise by the fight he had with his wife, also thought he was in. After hearing this evidence John Kelly was acquitted.

At their trial in early August Barry and Barratt did everything they could to 'get off the hook'. First their defence counsel alleged that Henry Culshaw had not been healthy in the first place which was why 'mortification' had set in. Henry's brother, John Culshaw, a clogger, was called and he testified that Henry was very healthy. He'd seen him earlier in the night of the attack and he had been absolutely fine. Well, counsel argued, Henry had also had medical treatment which could have been given by an unskilled or incompetent doctor. The Judge was not impressed and pointed out that Culshaw would not have needed treatment in the first place had he not been beaten up. However he had to accept that neither Irishman had set out to kill Henry Culshaw. They had simply been spoiling for a good fight; wanted to give someone a good kicking; had not actually intended to kill anyone. On this basis, though Edward Barry and Peter Barratt were found guilty of manslaughter (albeit involuntary manslaughter), they were only sentenced to three months imprisonment with hard labour; not a severe punishment and hardly one to fit the crime.

Footnote

About a month before the trial it had been suggested that a public subscription should be raised for Henry Culshaw's mother, Mrs Martha Culshaw as she had been completely dependent upon her son before his death. Accordingly a notice was put in the *Bolton Chronicle* for the 10 July inviting donations to be made to the fund. By 25 September the paper was pleased to report that a total of £33.10s (approximately £1,750 today) had been raised, so she was not left with any means of support. Ladies in Mrs Culshaw's position would use the cash to purchase a sewing machine or some such similar tools of trade so that they had the means of earning an independent living and could put a roof over their head.

CHAPTER 10

The Jealousy of Thomas Davis
1871

Her face and one arm bore marks of a murderer's fingers...

Samuel Davis had been working down the coal pit all day and he was hungry. As he trudged home through the cool October evening to the cosy cottage in Breightmet, near Bolton where he lived, he wondered what his mother had got for tea. Although he was eighteen years old he lived at home. It was handy and he wasn't courting properly yet. The window blinds were drawn which was a bit odd he thought. His mother usually left them open until he arrived home. He lifted the latch to push open the door but it seemed to be wedged. Putting his shoulder against it he practically fell into the living room as a pair of scissors clattered to the floor. His father was sitting in his usual chair near the fireplace, but he seemed to be drooped forward, his hands touching his stockinged feet. His cap lay on the floor. Alarmed, Samuel went over to his father and put both hands on his shoulders, gently levering him to an upright position. Then he drew back in horror. His father's throat had been cut. He looked down at the floor. It was covered in blood.

Uttering a strangled cry Samuel ran to his next door neighbour, James Allen, and gasped out his news. James rushed back to the house with him. It was only then that Samuel realised that his mother and his young nephew were missing. James and Samuel ran up the stairs together. Jane Davis was lying dead in bed with something like a towel tied tightly around her throat. She was still in her night-dress and had obviously been attacked while she was asleep. There were signs of a severe struggle. The bedclothes were in disarray and her head lolled off the bed. Her face and one arm bore marks of a murderer's fingers and there was discoloration over her eyes.

In the next room they found Samuel's four-year-old nephew,

Robert Nuttall, cowering in bed. He said he'd not heard his grandmother making any unusual noises but when she'd not come to get him up for his breakfast he'd gone downstairs and seen his grandfather being sick. Frightened, he'd scuttled back to bed. He had seen James Allen from his window and shouted to him but the old man appeared not to hear him so he'd stayed in the room all day waiting for someone to come for him. James Allen was in fact profoundly deaf and there was no way he would have heard the little boy shouting for help from inside the house.

After the discovery of his parents' bodies Samuel changed out of his colliers clothes and went to Tong Fold to tell his brothers what had happened. A neighbour named Alice Horrocks came in to lay out Jane and Thomas. While she was laying out Thomas she was surprised to discover three bullets and some gun powder in a small tin in Thomas's trouser pockets. Samuel didn't even know that his father possessed a gun and threw the bullets away. Alice was even more surprised when she came to lay out Jane for a common single barrel

Thomas brooded jealously over his wife, Jane, and wondered what would happen were he to die before her. Hannah Niblett

pistol, loaded and capped, was found amongst the tangled bedclothes in which Jane was lying.

It was now left to the police and the Coroner to piece together what had happened. Jane Davis was fifty-one years of age; her husband Thomas was fifty-two. They had been married for about thirty years and had eight children: five sons and three daughters; the youngest, Nancy, a girl of thirteen. Four of their children were married and four still lived at home. Thomas was not the father of the eldest son who was named Henry Nuttall. Henry lived at Tong and had been a widower for about two and a half years; so his young son, Robert, lived with Henry's mother and step father.

That morning Samuel had left for work at Jethro Scowcroft's Tong Colliery at around five-fifteen. Samuel's brother, John, who worked at Breightmet Colliery, left for work soon afterwards. The two girls, Alice and Nancy, who both worked at Hampson's Mill, were the last to leave the cottage at twenty to six, leaving their parents asleep in bed. The four children still living with Jane and Thomas all slept in the same room while Robert had the 'boy's bed' underneath the windowsill.

Thomas worked at home weaving counterpanes. He had been in bad health for a year or two and was very depressed. He had at one point threatened to hang himself. Dr Roberts was treating him. Thomas had not taken anything so far as he knew and the doctor described him as 'steady'. There were no financial worries as the children were all in work, and they were quite comfortably off, so Thomas could choose whether or not to work. However, Esther Schofield, a neighbour, would testify that on the Monday before the tragedy Thomas had come to her to ask for some castor oil because he 'was poorly and full of troubles'.

The inquest was held on Saturday, 28 October, at the *Starkie Arms Inn* on Tong Moor, owned by Mrs Jane Gorse. Coroner J Broughton-Edge and his jury of twelve good men and true sat solemnly in a makeshift courtroom to try and determine the truth of what had taken place in the Thomas's cottage just two days before.

Mr Cawthorne, the surgeon, had examined Jane and Thomas Davis on the Thursday evening and pronounced both of them to be dead. He said that Jane had been dead for between six and eight hours. Her face and her throat were livid and discoloured. A coloured handkerchief (which Jane wore instead of a night-cap) was tied loosely around her neck under a piece of bedquilt which had been tightly knotted under her larynx. She had been strangled.

Thomas's gullet, windpipe and muscles had been severed with a knife and death would have been fairly instantaneous. The razor with which his throat had been cut had been lying on a table near the window. Mr Cawthorne said that Thomas's throat had obviously been cut while standing at the table because there was a trail of blood from the table to the chair as well as the pool of blood on the floor around the chair.

Given that the door had been wedged shut with a pair of scissors on the inside; there was no sign of a break-in; and Thomas would have just had time to reach his chair before collapsing; the surgeon concluded that Thomas had committed suicide. In which case it was regrettably obvious that he had killed his wife first and then killed himself.

The question was why. Jane and Thomas Davis appeared to have had an amicable enough marriage with few arguments and he had never been known to threaten her, at least in public. Jane was strong, vigorous and healthy, and looked after her husband when he was ill. There were no financial worries. It was a mystery altogether why Thomas should have suddenly killed his wife and then himself.

When family members were questioned, however, it appeared that there had been signs of dissension between Jane and Thomas. Alice Davis said that about a month beforehand there had been some sort of a quarrel between Thomas and Jane. Although she thought they had resolved their quarrel there was still 'some sulking' in the evenings. The night before their deaths Alice had gone to bed at about twenty to ten. Her mother was sitting at the table sewing. Her father was still weaving. There wasn't much conversation between them but they had seemed amicable enough.

Henry Nuttall said that about eighteen months before Jane and Thomas had had a violent quarrel. Thomas had pulled Jane off her chair by her hair and give her a black eye. The problem at that time had been that Henry was living with them (he had only been a widower for a year by then) and Thomas had become angry and jealous because he thought that Henry was getting or purchasing goods in their name. Henry described Thomas as a passionate man with a hasty temper. The razor used to cut Thomas's throat had belonged to Henry. Ann Haslam, Jane's sister, thought Thomas was a jealous man. She said that he had told her that when women had finished having their children they strayed. He knew he was in poor health and that he would probably die before Jane; and he could not bear to think of her re-marrying. They had recently quarrelled over a man named Mark Allen. When they had lived in Roscoe Fold about eighteen months previously Thomas had been despondent on account of some other jealousy. Ann said that when the children were not there Thomas often quarrelled with Jane because of some perceived jealousy.

None of the family had known that there was a gun in the house. Was it possible that Jane had feared for her life and kept the loaded pistol under her pillow? Jane was a strong woman so how could Thomas have overpowered her and strangled her? It was surmised that he had used the element of surprise. Their bed was low, only eighteen inches from the ground. He would have waited until the house was empty (except for the young child who was asleep in the next room and obviously didn't count in Thomas's eyes) and then while Jane was still asleep he had knelt on her and tied the strip of quilt around her neck, pulling it tight. All of this woke Jane, of course, but although she struggled wildly she would have been at a severe disadvantage.

The hearing lasted four hours as it became clear what must have happened. The cause was a passionate jealous man in poor health who loved his wife but could not bear to think of her living without him or marrying another man after his death. These thoughts had sent him spiralling into a serious depression and in desperation he had finally killed both himself and his wife. The Coroner's jury returned a verdict of wilful murder followed by suicide whilst temporarily of unsound mind. It was a tragic end to what seemed to have been an otherwise successful marriage.

CHAPTER 11

Most Horrible Circumstance
1831

*In the flash of light following the noise of the shot
he saw a figure falling*

On a June evening in 1831 three people were walking home alongside the Bury, Bolton and Manchester Canal. Samuel Hopkinson, a crofter from Raikes who lived at Howell Brow in Tonge-with-Haulgh near Bolton, his wife Mary, and their friend, Betty Partington, had been to a funeral at Ringley Chapel. The walk was quite a long one and Samuel was pleased that they'd left the children at home. It was getting late and as they neared the bridge by Fogg's Colliery Betty said she was thirsty and wanted to stop off at the *Farmers Arms*. Mary agreed and told Betty she could murder a brandy and water. There had obviously been an eavesdropper to this conversation for suddenly a jeering voice on the far side of the canal said 'I'll give you a brandy and water!' John McGowan, the owner of the voice, then came across the bridge and stood in front of the women, demanding to know their business. He was the night watchman at Fogg's and he was armed. An argument broke out and there was a lot of shouting. McGowan raised his pistol and ordered them to leave the tow path. Mary was incensed. 'I have as much right as thee to stand on the canal bank!' she yelled. 'Fire! I can stand my corner!' There was a single shot and Mary Hopkinson collapsed onto the ground.

James Smith, a bedquilt weaver, was walking home along the canal bank when he saw a number of people on the canal bridge ahead of him. He could hear their raised voices and then he heard a single shot. In the flash of light following the noise of the shot he saw a figure falling. There was a moment's silence, then the sound of footsteps hurrying away and a woman's voice shouting 'Murderer!' James broke into a run. A man brushed past him and James looked at him but neither of them spoke. A minute later he stood beside the group. At his feet a woman lay on the ground, one side of her face blackened with powder. On asking what had happened Betty Partington told him that the man he'd just passed had shot Mary.

James Smith helped Samuel Hopkinson as he tried to move his wife. At this point John McGowan returned. They asked him to find assistance immediately as he had just shot Mary. To their amazement McGowan denied shooting her. He was holding a gun in his hand with a bayonet fixed on the end. Betty turned on him furiously and challenged him about the shooting. He turned to her with a look of contempt and said if she didn't hold her tongue he'd shoot her. John Hickson, a bleacher, was returning home from work at about eleven twenty when he heard a commotion and saw the little group on the bridge. He went across and asked what was to do. McGowan threatened to shoot Hickson as well before shouldering his weapon; then he turned on his heel and strode off into the darkness. Betty was shocked and distressed but somehow she, Samuel and James got Mary to the *Farmers Arms* some half a mile distant from the bridge. They called for a doctor, but it was too late. Mary Hopkinson died three days later in the early hours of Friday, 17 June.

John McGowan was arrested. He was an Irish pensioner who had managed to obtain a post as night watchman at Fogg's colliery, he said, and on the night in question he'd been on duty with two other night watchmen, William Howe and Meredith Trotter. They had both been arrested the day after McGowan. All three had been recommended to Mr Williams at the colliery by the Manchester Police. It was normal to discharge pistols every night as practice but firing at people was always a last resort in case it provoked another turn-out by the colliers. On the night in question pistols were fired in practice as usual and McGowan claimed that Mary Hopkinson had fainted with fright. He had definitely not shot her.

The Coroner's inquest was held at the *Farmers Arms* in Tonge-with-Haulgh about a mile from Bolton town centre on the 18 June. A large and angry crowd had gathered, wanting to get their hands on McGowan. The Coroner's jury of sixteen local tradesmen was sworn in at two o'clock but reporters were excluded from the proceedings. Betty Partington was the first to give evidence and identified McGowan as the man who shot and killed Mary Hopkinson. McGowan had changed his story slightly by this time. At first he'd insisted that Mary had simply fainted from fright. Now he simply denied knowing that he had injured her in any way. He admitted to seeing the group on the footpath and that they appeared to be drunk. He'd shouted a warning because there had been trouble in the vicinity of late but he had not fired at her.

Mr Mallet the surgeon called to tend Mary's injuries said that she had died from a single gunshot wound to her head. The bullet had been flattened by the force with which it had struck the bone and her face was blackened with powder on one side indicating that she had been shot at close range.

James Smith identified McGowan as the man who had brushed past him as he ran to the scene of the tragedy. He also said that McGowan had returned to the scene, still armed, and they'd asked him to go for assistance because he was the man who had shot Mary. He had refused to do so and had left them there to cope as best they could.

John Hickson, a bleacher, said he had found McGowan pointing his gun at Betty Partington and when he intervened McGowan had threatened him as well before shouldering his gun and walking away. Hickson had helped to carry Mary Hopkinson to Smithy Brow and then retraced his steps home. When he reached the bridge again he was once more challenged by McGowan.

Mrs Jones, the proprietress at the colliery, testified that she had heard a shot and came out to see what had happened. McGowan had told her that some people had been abusive and he had fired a warning shot in the air. One woman had fainted with fright. Mrs Jones said that shots at night were common since the unrest among the colliers and she thought nothing more of it.

The inquest was then adjourned and resumed the following Wednesday at the *Swan Hotel* in Bolton. McGowan had been stoned as he left the first part of the inquest and security was increased. Samuel Hopkinson corroborated Betty Partington's evidence. Mary had not spoken again after she was shot. She had not fainted. McGowan had shot her at point blank range.

Samuel and Mary had several children and Hopkinson cursed McGowan for leaving them motherless. At this point Meredith Trotter, hearing the commotion, had arrived at the scene and taken McGowan away.

A lady named Rachel Ripley had been on the Fogg's colliery side of the canal that night. She had heard sounds of a quarrel and woman's raised voice saying that she had as much right to stand on the canal bank as anyone else. Then she'd heard a gunshot. Immediately afterwards she saw McGowan standing in front of Mrs Jones's house shouting 'All's well!'

The Coroner's jury then retired to consider their verdict. Trotter and Howe were discharged since there was no evidence against them. McGowan was found guilty of wilful murder and committed for trial at Lancaster assizes. The following Sunday Mary Hopkinson was buried at the Parish Church of St Peter in Bolton and her funeral was attended by a crowd of five hundred people.

McGowan's trial took place on Saturday, 13 August at Lancaster Castle. He was found guilty of killing Mary Hopkinson by firing a blunderbuss (which was also carrying a double bayonet) at her and he was sentenced to be executed at eight o'clock on the morning of Monday, 15 August. A group of barristers, magistrates, lawyers and even some of the jurors felt the sentence was too harsh however. They felt he had been provoked by an insolent woman who was probably drunk and it was his misfortune that his shot had actually killed her. As a result, McGowan's sentence was commuted at dawn on the Monday morning to one of transportation for life.

CHAPTER 12

The Good Lord of Bolton
1487

...on the wrong side at the wrong time.

The old adage 'life isn't fair' could have been felt no more keenly than by Sir Thomas Pilkington, a member of the illustrious Pilkington family of Lancashire, who fell from grace in a spectacular manner because he happened to be 'on the wrong side at the wrong time.'

The Pilkington family had owned lands in the Bolton area since the days of William the Conqueror in the eleventh century. Stand Hall, or as it was known locally, Pilkington Tower, was their family seat. The first Hall was built around AD 1110. The second Hall was built in the thirteenth century and stood about one hundred yards to the east of the original Hall and remained the home of the family until the Wars of the Roses. It was during the fourteenth century that:

> *... from the Ferrers the Manor of Bolton passed by marriage to the Pilkingtons...one of the most powerful and distinguished families of that period...not only of Lancashire, but of the whole country...*

> (Scholes, James, *History of Bolton*, 1892)

Sir Thomas Pilkington was descended from Sir Roger Pilkington, one of two Knights of the Shire in 1366. He was styled 'the good Lord of Bury' and he was also 'a good Lord of Bolton'. Sir Thomas held the office of Sherriff of Lancashire several times between 1463-1487. He married Margaret Harrington of Hornby Castle, the '...co-heiress of Sir Richard Harrington and relict of Sir Christopher Hulton of Farnworth...' Sir Thomas was held in high esteem in Lancashire and he was much involved in civic life there.

However, when war broke out between the 'Red Rose of Lancashire' (emblem of Henry Tudor) and the 'White Rose of York' (emblem of the reigning King Richard III) Sir Thomas chose to support Richard III, the 'White Rose', in the Wars of the Roses. He might have been expected, perhaps, to have favoured the side of his own county, but many saw Henry Tudor as an upstart and believed that Richard III was the rightful king, and Sir Thomas Pilkington was among them.

He fought valiantly for Richard's cause but at the Battle of Bosworth Field on 22 August 1485, Richard was killed and Henry Tudor assumed the crown, styling himself Henry VII of England. Henry would brook no opposition and punished Richard's supporters viciously. Many were beheaded. Although he escaped with his life, Sir Thomas was ordered to forfeit all his lands in Lancashire to the Crown on 17 September 1485. The lands were then given as a reward to Thomas, Lord Stanley (Earl of Derby), who, after Richard's death, had placed the king's golden circlet on the head of Henry VII.

Outraged, impoverished, humiliated and furious, Sir Thomas, and others who had been treated in a like manner,

A neighbouring manor house to Stand Hall, Turton Tower came into the possession of the Orrell family at about the same time Sir Thomas lost Stand Hall. The author

plotted a Yorkist rebellion against the hated Tudor king. In 1487 a country lad named Lambert Simnel was paraded by the Yorkists as Edward Plantagenet, son of Richard III, who would have had a far more legitimate claim to the throne than Henry Tudor, a man of Welsh descent from the rebel Owen Tudor.

Henry, intelligent and astute, had expected some retaliation from the defeated and dispossessed Yorkists. He quickly realised that Lambert Simnel was an impostor and marshalled his forces. On 6 June 1487 the 'warring roses' met again and a fierce battle was fought on Stoke Field near Newark. Henry Tudor triumphed once more and Lambert Simnel was captured and taken prisoner. This time Sir Thomas didn't escape. He was killed in the battle, a tragic end to the story of a man who had fought for and lost everything. 'The winner takes all', and Henry Tudor did, but history had the last laugh. While the dynasty which Henry founded lasted less than a hundred and twenty years, the Pilkington dynasty (if not Sir Thomas) flourished and continues to do so; the name is probably best known in modern times for high quality Pilkington Glass manufacture.

All that remains of Sir Thomas Pilkington's estate is a name-plate and a gutted shell in the middle of a modern housing development. The author

CHAPTER **13**

Once a Jolly Clogger
1858

Thomas was lying on the floor, a large gash in his throat from which blood was pouring into the chamber pot over which he was leaning.

Of all the murders and foul deeds related in this book this one stands out because the reasons which lay behind it were not grinding poverty, drunken violence, rage, greed, revenge, jealousy, or any other base motive; rather desperation and heartbreak, and what the murderer perceived to be altruistic motives. Murder is never altruistic but it is hard to read this story without feeling some sympathy for what lay behind it.

Thomas Jolly was a master clogger. He was a literate, sensible, man who earned a comfortable living making clogs. When he married it was for love and he doted on his wife. She was a bonnet maker and had lived at Bradshaw Chapel before her marriage. They had two children William and Mary. The family had lived in Chorley, Bradshaw and Bolton before moving to Horwood, two miles north east of Bolton. Their cottage in Horwood was set midway down Seven Stars Row,

The Crofters Arms *lies to the centre of Bradshaw, from where Mrs Jolly came, and where the Jolly family lived for a while.* The author

Bradshaw churchyard, near Bolton, where Thomas Jolly's wife was buried before he went on his murderous spree. The author

'... a clump of houses in Leegate Lane known as the hillock...' about quarter of a mile from Bradshaw Church. The house was 'clean and well furnished' and the family should have been happy there.

The day before they were due to move in the early spring of 1858, tragedy struck. Mrs Jolly died in Bolton. Neither her name nor the cause of her death is recorded but she died at a time when consumption (tuberculosis) was the biggest killer. She was buried at Bradshaw Chapel. Thomas was absolutely devastated. He was only thirty-two and his wife had been younger. Somehow he managed to move himself and their grieving children, Mary now aged three and William, five years old, to Horwood. The children missed their mother but Thomas was known as '...a kind and indulgent parent, though sometimes irritable...' and did his best for them.

He arranged for his next door neighbour, Nancy Hampson, to cook, clean and wash for the family, and to mind the children when he was working. Often they played out on the 'fold'. Each week-day Thomas sent the children to a nearby infants' school run by Mrs Chadwick, his late wife's step-mother. School dinners were not provided and so the children came home for a meal at lunchtime.

Thomas had a problem, however. Before his wife's death he had a habit of 'tippling'; that is he drank regularly but not heavily. It was not seen as a problem since most men drank and the pub was a social gathering place where business was done as well as exchanging gossip. After Mrs Jolly died Thomas, '...often wild and in great grief...', started to drink a great deal. He 'fuddled' continuously and neglected his work. When drunk Thomas could become violent and irrational. People began to talk. Mrs Hampson remonstrated with him and, when he was sober, Thomas would promise to mend his ways.

He tried to keep his promise. On 7 July that year he joined Bolton Temperance Progression Society. When he received his pledge card he hung it on the wall of his shop and told everyone he'd given up drinking. Thomas was 'full of troubles' though and within three weeks he was drinking heavily again.

On Wednesday, 8 August Thomas went to Bolton to purchase a quantity of nails and two dozen clog soles. Between ten and eleven o'clock that morning he locked his cottage door and gave the key to Mrs Hampson, telling her that if the children came home from school before he was back she was to give them something to eat. She agreed and pocketed the key.

Mary and William arrived home shortly after midday. Mrs Hampson gave them some bread and butter and sent them out to play. Thomas returned about twelve thirty and collected the children. Mrs Hampson went to his house soon afterwards and found him putting potatoes on the fire for dinner. Five minutes later she went back and Jolly was sitting at the table, his head resting on his hand, looking completely dejected. She spoke to him and, getting no answer, repeated what she had said. He

A nineteenth century cobbled lane, near Horwood. The author

lifted his head and looked at her and the 'wild fiendish expression' on his face frightened her so much that she ran back to her own house.

A little while later, at about one o'clock, she heard him calling the children to their dinner. He asked her for a pickled herring for them to eat with their potatoes. She gave him one though the children didn't like pickled herring and, it was subsequently discovered, hadn't eaten it. After dinner she saw him in the yard washing out the 'chamber utensils' (pots kept under the bed before the days of inside toilets). He took one upstairs and left the other one in the back kitchen.

Around one forty five a little girl came from the school to ask why Mary and William hadn't returned after dinner. Mrs Chadwick, the teacher, knowing that Thomas 'often went on the spree', was concerned. The child had tried both the front and back door but they had appeared to be locked so she went next door to Mrs Hampson. Mrs Hampson said she hadn't seen them and went to Thomas's house . She looked through the window first. She could see Thomas's apron on the table and all their clogs at the foot of the stairs. Mrs Hampson knew that he was in the habit of going to bed with the children sometimes so she tried the back door. At first it seemed shut fast but she pushed hard and finally the door gave way and she opened it.

There was no one downstairs but Mrs Hampson could hear a strange sound, a 'dismal noise', so she went to the stairs and shouted 'Hello!' She was answered by a guttural sound as though someone was suffocating. She screamed and ran for help to Thomas Holt, a shopkeeper who lived on the other side of the Jolly house higher up the lane. Holt ran into Thomas's cottage and up the stairs. Thomas was lying on the floor, a large gash in his throat from which blood was streaming into the chamber pot over which he was leaning. Holt gasped. 'Oh Thomas!' he said. 'What have you done?'

He knelt beside Thomas and tried to help him, but Thomas, who could not speak, jerked Holt's arm away and crashed to the floor.

Holt ran downstairs, out of the cottage, into the *Seven Stars* beer house and blurted out what had happened. Neighbour

James Tootal, a local book keeper, rushed back to Thomas's house with Holt. Thomas Jolly lay on the floor close to death. Only then did they remember the children and looked quickly around for them. Little Mary lay dead on the bed with her throat slashed right across. There was no sign of William. Then they heard a kind of gurgling whimper and discovered William lying moaning under the bed with deep gashes to his throat and fingers.

PC William Gillibrand had by this time arrived on the scene and he sent at once for Bolton surgeon Mr Cawthorne. The surgeon did not arrive until nearly three o'clock. By this time Thomas Jolly was dead, his razor lying on the floor beside him. He had '...severed his windpipe, gullet and all soft parts back to his spine...' In short he'd almost decapitated himself. Mary lay with her head hanging downwards off the bed. The walls were spattered with blood and large pools of blood lay on the floor. The place looked more like an abattoir than a bedroom.

William was, however, still alive. He had lost a lot of blood from the two wounds, each two inches long, on the left-hand side of his neck, and another across his windpipe. He also had a wound on his left cheek and cuts on the forefinger and thumb of one hand. The surgeon dressed his wounds as best he could and William was taken to neighbour Ann Relph's house where he was put to bed. His life hung in the balance for a while and Ann Relph nursed him devotedly for several weeks

William eventually made a full recovery and he was able to give an account of what had happened that dreadful day. It was a sad and pathetic tale that he told:

...after dinner Father took our clogs off and took off his own clogs and said that we would all go to bed together. When we got upstairs Mary said 'Daddy, what are we all going to bed so soon for?

Father replied that 'we were going to our everlasting home.'

We all got into bed together. Suddenly Father got up, took hold of Mary, held her at the side of the bed and cut her throat. She tried to scream but she just gurgled. Then he turned and went for me. We struggled a lot and he cut my fingers. I tried to call out but he cut my cheek and my neck. He had a sort of wild look and he was breathing very fast and sweating a lot. He dropped me on the bed. I was very frightened. I slid off the bed and crawled underneath it to hide from him. Then he knelt on the floor and cut his own throat...'

The inquest was held at the *Britannia Inn*, a quarter of a mile from the Jolly home, on Friday, 10 August, just two days after the tragedy. The Coroner's jury viewed the bodies of Thomas and Mary laid out on the bed in the upstairs room before the proceedings began. Thomas's movements on his last day were pieced together and it began to look as though the murder of his daughter and his suicide were premeditated.

Between five and six o'clock on the morning of Wednesday, 8 August Thomas had knocked up his landlord, farmer John Haslam, and paid him fifteen shillings due rent. Thomas told the farmer that he had made up his mind and would definitely be drinking no more. That morning Thomas also paid his 'milk score'. After returning from Bolton with his nails and clog soles Thomas drank a glass of ale at Abraham Bromiley's beer house in Leegate Lane. Abraham's wife, Alice, served him. She thought his appearance had been unusual and assumed he had been on 'on the spree'; so she asked him how soon he intended to go and look after his children. He had replied morosely that everybody was sorry for the children but no-one felt sorry for himself. Then he'd left.

Thomas Jolly had a sister who lived in Bolton. She said he'd been distressed recently when their father had been taken to a lunatic asylum. No-one had been aware before now that Thomas had had other family problems. Thomas's brother, Henry, who was aged twenty five and lived at Bank Top in Sharples, said that he didn't see much of Thomas, but he knew that their elder brothers, John and William, who lived in Chorley, had become concerned about Thomas's drinking and had talked to him on a few occasions. Thomas was constantly promising to mend his ways but it seemed that he just couldn't stay away from drink.

The jury returned a verdict that Thomas Jolly had killed his daughter and attempted to kill his son while labouring under a temporary insanity, and had afterwards taken his own life while in the same state of mind. A grief-stricken man at the end of his tether, he knew he could not stop drinking and he could not bear to go on living. He did not want to leave his young children for fear that they would be taken to the workhouse; and he may also have been afraid that his father's problems were hereditary.

Although there is no hard evidence, there is a feeling that Thomas Jolly was not particularly close to his family. He does not seemed to have turned to them when his wife died; preferring to move away and have his children looked after by a neighbour. There is no record of his sister from Bolton visiting him for she would surely have chatted with Mrs Hampson if she had done so. Then there is Henry's admission that he did not see much of his brother, although he didn't live far away; and it was left to his other brothers to come over from Chorley and 'speak to him about his drinking'.

What is known of Thomas's character when he was not drinking suggests that he was an intelligent man, a good craftsman, hardworking; a caring and kindly man who loved his wife and doted upon his children; a man who tried to do what was right. Then tragedy overtook him. His wife died and his father became seriously mentally ill. He was left alone with his grief and two young children to care for; seemingly without the benefit of a close family network. In the times in which Thomas lived men just did not talk about their problems ('no one felt sorry for him') and so he drank to kill the pain and tragically, along with that, killed himself and his adored small daughter.

Grief-stricken, Thomas Jolly killed his daughter, then paused briefly before killing himself. Hannah Niblett

CHAPTER 14

A Powder Called Quietness
1856

...intended for husbands who had drunk too much...

Daniel McMullan was not by nature an intemperate man but every two or three months he was given to serious bouts of drinking which could last two to three days. So when he complained to his doctor, Mr Dorian, on the Sunday evening just before Midsummer's Day in 1856, that he had been ill the previous day and had not gone to work, and that he felt sick after eating, the surgeon diagnosed indigestion and prescribed an antidote, in all likelihood peppermint, for his problem. It did not work. Daniel got worse. In fact the surgeon was 'astonished at the symptoms manifested', and he began to suspect that Daniel had been poisoned with something.

His suspicion deepened when, two days later, on Tuesday, 24 June, the McMullans's servant girl, Mary Ann Hulton, gave him a small packet which she had taken from the pocket of her mistress, Betsy McMullan, who was Daniel's wife. Later that day Mary brought him some tea which Betsy had made for Daniel to drink. Mr Dorian took the tea and the packet to Mr HH Watson, an analytical chemist who worked in Bolton. Tartarised antimony was discovered in both the tea and in the white powder which the packet had contained. Antimony is a metallic element which is poisonous when given in any quantity. Mr Dorian called in a second medical man, Dr Chadwick. Together they decided that Daniel should be placed under the care of a nurse so that he would eat or drink nothing except what, quite literally, the doctor had ordered.

However, a week later it had become obvious that Daniel was not going to recover and on Tuesday, 1 July, Mr Dorian and Dr Chadwick took their findings to Mr Harris, the local superintendent of police. Betsy was then arrested on suspicion

Deansgate, from an Edwardian Postcard. Many of these buildings date from the Victorian period. Author's collection

of poisoning her husband. Nurse Sledden from Astley Bridge had been appointed to care for Daniel and she had remained with her charge night and day from 27-30 June until Mary Lee took over for what proved to be the last two days of Daniel's life. However, the case proved to be anything but the straightforward matter it had seemed. Betsy admitted at once that she had purchased 'a powder called quietness', intended for husbands who had drunk too much, from Mr JR Simpson, a druggist in Deansgate. The powder was said to cure them after 'a fuddle' and she had given her husband some of this powder when he had returned home from his latest drinking spree. The police called on Mr Simpson who agreed that he had sold some of this powder to Betsy McMullan and gave them a sample. The powder contained five grains of tartarised antimony and fifteen grains of cream of tartar. Mr Simpson told the police that he always gave strict instructions that this powder was to be administered in four or five doses; never all at once.

Mary Ann Hulton claimed however that Mr McMullan had been suffering from periods of sickness for months. She said that she had also been sent to get 'a powder of quietness' but she had gone to Mr Ratcliffe who had refused to sell her such a thing. During the last two or three months, she said, Mr McMullan had been sick more frequently and she had seen

Deansgate today, showing former Victorian shops and houses, including former druggists. The author

Mrs McMullan on several occasions putting white powder from a packet, which she kept in her pocket, into broth, tea, milk and medicine intended for Mr McMullan. Recently, while Mrs McMullan was asleep in a state of intoxication, she had made so bold as to look in Mrs McMullan's pocket where she found the white powder which she had handed over to Mr Dorian.

Mary Ann told the police that Mr McMullan was a quiet well disposed man who had gone on three serious drinking bouts in the nine months she had lived in the house. Each drinking session lasted about three days. After he 'had come off a fuddle' he was always poorly but he was not in the habit of taking medicines. His last bout had been from Saturday, 7 June to Wednesday, 11 June. When he had recovered he had attended to his shop until he was taken poorly the following Friday, had got worse on the Saturday, and had finally called in his doctor at around five or six o'clcock on the Sunday.

The story which began to emerge was complicated and not altogether edifying. Daniel McMullan was forty-three-years-old; 'a man of spare habit of body, not strong, and not an entirely temperate person...who had outbreaks of drinking, which lasted two or three days, once every two or three months...'. By trade he was a spinner but he later became a flour dealer and had a shop at 32 Moor Lane in Bolton. His wife, Betsy, helped out in the shop. A tradesman's daughter, she was 'a goodly looking person of above average height...aged thirty-eight...with an imperfect education...' The couple had been married for a number of years and lived in Blackburn Street just off Moor Lane. They had had several children 'but none were now living', and the marriage had been unhappy for some time. Betsy McMullan, it was said, had a 'great fondness for whisky' and drank most days and nights. She also had a penchant for fortune tellers of which Daniel disapproved. She told their former next door neighbour, John Lee (a carder and overlooker in one of the Bolton mills), that she had consulted a fortune teller about a man with whom she had 'walked out' (courted) before she knew Daniel and said that she would 'rather have his [the man she'd courted] little finger than Dan's whole body...'

Betsy McMullan was alleged to be having an affair with a local married man named Peter who worked at Hicks Foundry, drank in the *Three Tuns* public house opposite the McMullan house, and who seemed to spend a good deal of time in the McMullan kitchen. The affair was not proved but Daniel got to hear of the rumours. On 7 June Betsy could not work in the shop as usual because she had received 'a blow in the face or a fall...' so Daniel worked there on his own. That evening he went across to the Three Tuns and had a furious row with Peter. Afterwards Daniel went to the *Archduke* public house and got, in modern jargon, 'blind drunk and absolutely legless.' By about midnight, when he had not returned home, Betsy, by now very drunk herself, and Mary Ann went looking for him. When they found him, still in the *Archduke*, there was a violent quarrel, and Betsy attacked him with a knife and a rolling pin she grabbed from the kitchen which adjoined the bar of the *Archduke*. She was too drunk to be able to hurt Daniel and he disarmed her easily. They both calmed down and then spent

Moor Lane, Bolton, today, showing where Daniel McMullan had his flour shop at no 32. The author

Moor Lane, showing the spire of St Paul's church. The author

the next two or three hours drinking together in the *Archduke* while a sober and patient Mary Ann sat on a chair and waited for them to be ready to go home. Around four o'clock in the morning Betsy and Daniel finally staggered into the street and there was another violent quarrel. Daniel then stormed off, leaving Mary to assist Betsy home. Mary Ann got her back to the house, washed and undressed her and put her to bed; and it was then that she had taken the powder from Betsy's pocket.

Mary Ann was worried. Over the last three months she had often seen Betsy adding powder to Daniel's food in the pantry. She would add it to a tasty broth or to porridge which she would then serve with treacle and buttermilk to disguise the taste. During those three months Betsy would often send Mary Ann into the shop while she dished up food. Daniel wasn't drinking at this time and, even more worryingly, he'd not been sick before as he constantly seemed to be at present. So she'd voiced her concerns to the doctor. Then on Friday, 27 June Betsy had sent her to buy some tripe. Mary Ann was only gone a few minutes and when she returned Betsy was busy with a customer in the shop. Mary Ann took the tripe into the pantry and noticed a glass gill cup 'with something in it.' She took the sediment to give to the doctor. At four o'clock that same day Betsy gave Mary Ann some tea to take up for Daniel to drink. Mary Ann only gave Daniel the top and preserved the dregs. These she gave to the doctor as well. On analysis it was discovered that both samples contained pure antimony.

Daniel McMullan, delirious and jaundiced, died at two in the morning on 2 July 1856. The post-mortem was held at two o'clock that afternoon. Cause of death was determined as due to inflammation of the mucus membrane of the stomach, the bowel and the small intestine, which could have been due to natural causes although there was nothing to suggest that they were. The inquest was told that the symptoms which Daniel suffered: sickness, burning pain, faintness and dizziness; could have been caused by natural disease. There was no proof. The classic textbook symptoms of antimony poisoning: diarrhoea, constriction of the throat and spasms; were not present. There was however, the circumstantial evidence and Mary Ann's testimony to consider; and there was also the fact that Betsy had admitted giving Daniel the powder containing antimony.

James Rowland Simpson, druggist and grocer of Deansgate, Bolton, was called to give evidence at the inquest. He agreed that the antimony powders were dangerous and designed to be used with caution. They were called 'tartar emetic powders' but they were commonly known as 'quietness powders'. Directions were not written or printed on the packets but purchasers were told to use them with caution and over a number of doses. He said that only women whose husbands had 'been on the spree' ever asked for them as they were intended to 'cause sickness and throw up the dregs of drink'. He never sold any to children or to young people; only to adults and married women.

More importantly there was the matter of the insurance

Daniel and Betsy McMullan quarrelled drunkenly in the street. Hannah Niblett

money. John Thornton, who lived in Great Bolton, worked as an insurance agent for the Prince of Wales Life Insurance Company in Bolton. Daniel had taken out an insurance policy of £100 (current value £4,903.33) in January 1855 on the joint lives of himself and Betsy, payable to the survivor. Six quarters' premiums were required to be paid up before it became effective and Daniel had paid the last one in April 1856. When he'd called at the house on Tuesday, 1 July 1856 (the day before Daniel's death) he had been asked to fetch the Company's medical referee to the house. This he had done but the medical referee had been excluded from the post mortem. Dr Chadwick was of the firm opinion that the policy offered an ideal motive for Betsy to poison her husband.

The Coroner summed up by saying that the powder had been administered when the deceased was not drunk, and without his knowledge, and could have caused or accelerated death. Even if some symptoms of antimony poisoning were missing, he considered that the antimony must have been a contributing factor, especially as there was no proof of natural disease. After just twenty five-minutes the Coroner's Jury returned a verdict of wilful murder against Betsy and she was committed for trial at Liverpool. The Jury also condemned the random selling and dispensing of powders such as that which Betsy was accused of administering to her husband.

Betsy was not in the Court to hear the verdict. Large crowds had gathered outside, and it was very plain that their sympathies did not lie with Betsy, so for her own safety she had been confined in an upper room. She could see the crowds from her window. She was much affected and desperately maintained that she was innocent. When her father came to tell her the verdict she wept. It was midnight before the crowd dispersed and she could be moved. She was taken to the star chamber at the old lock-ups where she spent a short time with her father, step-mother, brother and sister, and Daniel's brother before going to her bed.

Betsy could neither sleep nor eat. Next morning she rose at five and managed to take only a cup of tea before she was taken to Chequerbent Station on the LNWR line to catch the seven-ten train to Liverpool where she would be held at

Kirkdale awaiting her trial. In order not to excite attention, her father met the party in Derby Street so that he could accompany her to Kirkdale. Daniel was buried on Friday afternoon, 11 July 1856, at the Roman Catholic chapel in Pilkington Street. His funeral was attended by large crowds of mourners; but Betsy was not allowed to attend.

Betsy McMullan's trial began in August and Mr Monk was appointed to defend her. The trial was a little delayed because of the need to take evidence from a witness too ill to attend court. Elizabeth Hilton, a widow who lived near the *Britannia* public house in Moor Lane, was dying of consumption (tuberculosis). Mary Ann said that when she'd first discovered the powder in Betsy's pocket she'd given it to her friend, Teresa Fitzgerald, who had simply kept the powder for a fortnight and did nothing about it. Mary Ann had then taken it to Mrs Hilton's house, because she knew that the doctor was calling on Mrs Hilton every day and she wanted the powder identified before she voiced her suspicions. Mary Ann only left the powder with Mrs Hilton overnight but the doctor had not called and so Mary Ann had retrieved the powder, still unidentified.

Nine members of Mrs Hilton's family lived in her cottage. Her youngest child was nineteen and they all went out to work so she was quite alone during the day. Mrs Hilton was lying in bed, too ill to move. Crowded around her bed were Mr Harris, the local Superintendent of Police; Robert Walsh, one of the Borough Magistrates; Mr Winder, Clerk to the Magistrates; Mr Briggs, Betsy's solicitor; Mr W Challinor, clerk to John Gaskell, the Borough Prosecutor; and Betsy McMullan herself, brought secretly to the house so as to avoid more public demonstrations. Betsy sobbed bitterly as Mrs Hilton gave her evidence. Taking the deposition of her evidence took just thirty-five minutes and then Betsy was smuggled out of the house and back to Liverpool; being taken, with her family, to meet the train at Lostock Junction in case someone should recognise her in Bolton.

Meanwhile, James Lomax was sent to photograph and survey Betsy's kitchen and to draw up plans of her house to show that a person in the pantry could easily be seen from the

Modern law courts in Bolton, on Moor Lane, next to the bus station. The author

kitchen, as Mary Ann had testified.

The trial began on 15 August 1856 at Liverpool Assizes. Betsy was '...attired in deep mourning and she wore a thick crepe veil partially thrown over her bonnet...' The case hinged mainly on the medical evidence and that of Mary Ann. The court was told that Mr Dorrian had initially treated Daniel for dyspepsia but he had quickly realised that it was something far more serious. Daniel had been given powders which, when analysed, were found to contain much antimony; so, after 27 June, neither wife nor servant were allowed to give him food or drink and Daniel had only received nourishment from the nurses. He had been a very sick man and he had actually died of sheer exhaustion. The post-mortem examination had revealed that his stomach and intestines were extremely swollen and the presence of antimony was discovered in his liver, kidneys and spleen; though not in his stomach or colon which would accord with the period before his death when the nurses prepared his food and drink.

Mary Ann Hutton was also carefully cross examined. She was a girl of Irish descent, born in County Kildare. Her father was a book keeper for the Grand Canal. She lived and worked with Mr Dunn, a married man, at Round Town near Dublin before moving into Dublin where she had lived and worked with Mr Casey (a pawnbroker) for three weeks; and before that with his next door neighbour (also a pawnbroker) for two months. She was 'of good character' and had come recommended to work for Mr and Mrs McMullan. They all seemed to live together amicably enough but it is tempting to wonder what Mary Ann really thought about her master and mistress's drinking and her mistress's supposed men friends. In court she painstakingly re-told her story. Although her evidence was pivotal to the fate of Betsy McMullan it was uncorroborated, but the Judge decided that this did not matter as Mary Ann was 'of a good character'.

Mary Ann McGill and her husband, Andrew McGill, kept the *Archduke* public house where Daniel and Betsy had drunk and fought together. They had witnessed the fight between the McMullans when Betsy had grabbed a knife from the knife box in the kitchen and then a rolling pin so that she could attack Daniel. Later Daniel had asked the McGills for a bed but was told to go home and sort matters out.

PC John Whitehead testified to the couple's earlier unhappiness with each other by saying he had witnessed a drunken fight between them about three months previously when they threw flour at each other and then Betsy had thrown a dish at Daniel.

Mary Cummins, a friend of Teresa Fitzgerald, now came forward to say that she had actually taken the white powder from Theresa's house to Mr Partington the druggists and asked if it was carbonate of soda, but she was told '…it was bad stuff, sickening stuff…' and that she must not use it.

It was a long trial and it seemed as though almost everyone who had ever known the McMullans was called to give evidence. Betsy's fate was sealed when the Judge, in his summing up, said that although the medical evidence was not conclusive that Daniel had died of antimony poisoning, he was nevertheless extremely unhappy about the fact that the antimony or 'quietness powders' had been administered to Daniel without his knowledge. The jury found Betsy guilty of manslaughter and she was sentenced to transportation for life. Her father and her female friends wept openly in the public gallery for she had indeed received a harsh sentence.

In the twenty-first century Betsy's conviction would be deemed unsafe based, as it was, on inconclusive medical evidence and uncorroborated witness statements, but Betsy McMullan was a victim of her times. She may or may not have intended to kill her husband; that is something that will never be known or satisfactorily proved; but the fact that she appeared to have harmed him, unintentionally or otherwise, condemned her completely in the eyes of the patriarchal society in which she lived. The law then said that a man could be charged with beating his dog but not with beating his wife. She was lucky to escape with her life and she knew it. Just over seventy years before, in 1772, Mary Hilton of Bolton had been convicted of poisoning her husband. She had been sentenced to be strangled and then burned at the stake.

Antimony was widely used by nineteenth century doctors as an emetic. It was believed that purging someone in this way would expel the problem that was troubling them. Mill workers who developed coughs through inhaling cotton dust were widely prescribed emetics so that they would be sick and throw up the detritus. If only it had been that simple. There is also the possibility that Daniel was simply allergic to antimony and the whole episode was just a tragic accident. Betsy had been candid enough. She had made no attempt to hide the fact of what she gave him. The druggist was at least equally culpable for selling dangerous substances with no warnings or written instructions for use. People can and do forget what they have been told; and Betsy had also had 'an imperfect education'.

Mary Ann may have suffered from a lurid imagination or she may have harboured a secret grudge. Why was the Judge so keen to believe Mary Ann's uncorroborated evidence and not to believe anything Betsy had said? What had made the McMullans so unhappy with each other? That they had had several children 'but none were now living' speaks volumes about tragedy and heartache. Perhaps Betsy, desperate, worn down by grief over her lost children and long lonely evenings spent drinking to kill the pain, did poison Daniel and hoped that she would remain undetected so she could collect her insurance money and continue her affair with the married Peter. There are far too many unknowns in this case; far too many loose ends; far too many unresolved questions; and the jury should really still be out on what actually did happen that long ago midsummer in the flour dealer's house on Moor Lane.

CHAPTER 15

Martyr at the Stake
1555

'Father in Heaven! Have mercy on me!'

In Deane Churchyard there stands a beautifully carved Celtic style cross set into a decorated block of stone. This is the George Marsh memorial cross, erected to man who died 450 years ago, but whose bravery in standing up for what he believed in earned him a place in the annals of national history as well as in Bolton history. He also had the distinction of being Bolton's only Christian martyr.

George Marsh was born in Deane in 1515, the son of a yeoman farmer. He received a decent enough education and then became a farmer himself. He married in 1540 but his wife died while their children were still young. It was a grievous blow to him and he turned to the Church for comfort. Deciding that he wanted to devote himself to religion he left his

Right: Memorial to George Marsh, Deane churchyard. The author

Below: Detail showing inscription. The author

The road to Deane and Deane Moor. The author

children in the care of his mother and went to study at Cambridge University. Fellow Boltonians, James and Leonard Pilkington, sons of Lord Pilkington of Rivington, were also studying there. So too were Thomas, Ralph and John Lever of Darcy Lever not far from Bolton.

The new Protestant teachings were much discussed and admired and Marsh's study of the New Testament earned him an appointment as a preaching minister in 1547 when Edward VI ascended the throne. Edward, like his father, Henry VIII, who had engineered the break with Rome and the Catholic religion in order to marry Anne Boleyn, was a firmly Protestant monarch. During his reign *The Book of Common Prayer* was written and the saying of Mass was forbidden. By 1551 Marsh's friend Thomas Lever, had been made master of St John's College in Cambridge. Marsh graduated around this time. He progressed rapidly, becoming first a curate and then, a deacon, preaching in London and Leicestershire rather than

Thomas Lever, Master of St John's College, Cambridge, was a friend of George Marsh, who died at the stake for his beliefs. He and his brothers, Ralph and John, lived in Darcy Lever, near Bolton. Author's collection

his home town of Bolton. Disaster, however, was just around the corner.

Edward VI had always been a sickly youth and in 1553 he died at the tender age of fifteen. His sister, Mary Tudor, succeeded him. She was the daughter of Henry VIII's first Queen, Catherine of Aragon, who was Spanish and a devoted Catholic; the Queen who had been put aside for Anne Boleyn and who had been separated from her beloved daughter for refusing to consent to a divorce. Like her mother, Mary was also a devout Catholic, and determined to return England to what she saw as the 'true faith'. Under Queen Mary, Thomas Lever's position was untenable and he, together with his brothers and the Pilkington brothers, fled abroad. George Marsh was urged to do the same, but first he wanted to see his family.

Mary Tudor married the Catholic King Phillip II of Spain. Under his influence she began to increase persecution of heretics (non Catholics) at home. Queen Mary is known as Bloody Mary because she sent over three hundred heretics,

Smithills Hall, where George Marsh was taken for interrogation and where he is said to have stamped his foot and left an impression on a flagstone. The author

including several bishops, to be burned at the stake during her six year reign. It was a reign of terror but it has to be seen within the context of her times. In Spain, her husband, Phillip II, would have 300 heretics burned at the stake in a single episode, and he tried to encourage Mary to be more harsh with dissenters than she was. Marsh was urged by his friends and colleagues to flee as quickly as he could but he had determined that he would see his children one last time before he left for an exile of indeterminate length.

Returning to Bolton proved to be a fatal mistake. His London preaching had brought him to the attention of the Catholic Earl of Derby, under whose jurisdiction Bolton lay, and in March 1554 George Marsh was arrested. He was accused of preaching false doctrines and taken before Justice Sir Roger Barton at Smithills Hall. The Hall, which dates from the fourteenth century, stands near woods two or three miles from Bolton. It is said that Marsh was taken to the Green Chamber for his interrogation. In a passageway near to the door of the present dining room there is an indentation in the flagstone. According to legend, Marsh stamped his foot during interrogation to emphasise his belief that his faith was the true faith and this indentation was his footprint, '...a miraculous impression...made upon the stone as a perpetual memorial of the injustice of his enemies which neither time nor labour can efface...'

Marsh was next taken to Lathom Hall. The present building dates from the 1720s and is not the one to which Marsh was taken. The Hall in which Marsh was interrogated by Robert Brassey and Richard Gerard, both Catholic priests, was so completely demolished that today the exact site is uncertain. The first Lathom Hall was undoubtedly an impressive place. The home of the Stanleys, it had eighteen towers and a twenty-four foot (7.4m) wide moat. Marsh refused to recant and was imprisoned at Chester. Bishop Choates visited him frequently and tried his hardest to persuade Marsh to recant but George Marsh insisted on remaining true to his beliefs although he knew the penalty for doing so.

He was sentenced to be burned at the stake on 24 April 1555 in Spital Broughton near Chester. On the morning of his execution he was given one last chance to save his life and asked to renounce his beliefs on oath. Marsh refused absolutely. He was tied to the stake and the fire was lit. It was an agonising death, a true martyr's death, and his last words are reputed to have been a desperate scream 'Father of Heaven! Have mercy on me!'

The dreadful irony of George Marsh's fate is that just three years later Queen Mary was dead. Her half sister, Elizabeth, the daughter of Henry VIII and Anne Boleyn, became Queen. Elizabeth I was a staunch Protestant who returned England at once to the Protestant faith and who would have admired George Marsh and his teachings. Had he fled abroad to save his life, his exile away from his beloved children would not have been so very long. However, his sacrifice, and that of his fellow sufferers in the flames, had longer lasting repercussions than even he could have dreamed. Since Queen Mary's time England has never again had a Catholic monarch and even in the twenty-first century it is still enshrined in the Constitution that the sovereign cannot be a believer in the Catholic faith.

Deane church, Bolton, where there is a memorial to George Marsh. Author's collection

CHAPTER 16

Parricide at Halliwell
1869

'that horse has killed my father!'

Thomas Bennett, who was thirty-nine, had lived with his son, Samuel, at Poole's Fold in Halliwell for about seven months. He was grateful to his landlord, a greengrocer named John Holt, for giving them a room. Samuel, his only child, wasn't easy sometimes. Not that it was his fault. He was said to be 'of weak mind'. Inherited it from his mother and she'd been in the Chester Asylum now for the last six years, ever since Samuel was about eleven. Thomas had not realised when he first married her and thought her funny little ways rather sweet, but then she'd got worse. As soon as he'd discovered the truth he made sure there were no more children. He'd not asked for sympathy; you looked after your own; but when she'd become a danger to herself he'd had no choice. The doctor had been straight with him and told him she wouldn't come home again. He'd shrugged, accepted it, and did his best to look after his son.

Thomas and Samuel Bennett both worked as labourers. It was easier to keep an eye on the boy that way. Thomas could always find someone to give him a bit of work. Samuel might have been 'simple minded' but he was a tall young man, strong, and willing to earn his keep. Father and son got on well enough most of the time but Samuel could become quarrelsome and quick tempered when he'd had a few beers. Thomas tried to keep him in check but it was difficult at times. Going to the pub for a drink and a bit of gossip and perhaps a game or two was about the only pleasure Thomas had in his life; and he'd rather Samuel was with him so that he could keep an eye on him.

On the last day of March 1869 John Holt decided he needed to go into Bolton. He liked Thomas; pity about the boy; and he asked the Bennetts if they'd like to go with him, maybe have a beer or two. They set off in the late afternoon and arrived in Bolton around four-thirty. Thomas and Samuel went off to have a drink while John Holt spent about an hour doing his business. He would then have a drink with the Bennetts before they left for home.

Thomas and his son had spent the previous hour drinking and had got into some kind of an argument. Holt's attention was caught by a commotion he'd heard a little earlier on as he was concluding his business; and turning round he saw Thomas and his son fighting in the street. He ran up and managed to calm both of them down. Then he suggested that they went to the *Squirrel* public house for a beer. The three men ordered a quart of beer and shared it between them, talking casually together, Holt trying to restore the peace.

When they left, however, it was obvious that father and son were still angry with each other. The three of them climbed onto John Holt's cart and set off. They stopped after a little while at the *Victory Inn* on Chorley Old Road and each drank a gill of beer together, before continuing their journey. John Holt was up front driving while Thomas and Samuel sat behind him. Shortly afterwards, they began quarrelling again. Suddenly Samuel gave a roar of rage, seized hold of his father and pitched him out of the cart. Thomas fell heavily onto the roadway, landing between the wheels of the cart so that the rear wheels then ran over him.

Samuel jumped down off the cart and ran to his father and began kicking him. Jan Rimmer, a joiner, who was passing by, ran over and told him to stop it. Samuel rounded on him and said 'I will serve you the same!' but he stopped, then lay down on the ground 'moaning and groaning'. Jan Rimmer and John Holt somehow managed to lift Thomas back onto the cart and Samuel got up off the ground and went to sit beside his father. They started off homewards again but they hadn't gone very far when Samuel became angry and excited. He jumped up and shouted 'Stop the cart! That horse has killed my father! That horse has killed my father!'

His conduct startled the horse and Holt lost control for a few moments. Samuel leapt off the cart and started kicking Holt and the horse, yelling 'That horse has killed my father! That horse has killed my father!' This was too much for the restive horse who shied and dragged the cart against a fence and a gate post, overturning it and spilling Thomas and the rest of the contents into the roadway. Thomas, who had been clearly badly hurt in the first fall, was now in a lot of pain. James Pendlebury, a farmer who knew John Holt, drew up behind them. It was decided that he would take Thomas home while John Holt righted his cart and retrieved his goods. John Bath, a bricklayer, who was passing gave Pendlebury and Jan Rimmer hand to lift the by now very badly injured Thomas on to Pendelbury's cart.

Samuel went to jump on the cart with him but was restrained by James Pendlebury. Samuel drew a knife and threatened him. 'I have told you! I will serve you the same! That horse has killed my father! ' Pendlebury and Rimmer disarmed him and told him to make his own way home. James Pendlebury then took Thomas home in his cart as slowly as he could but it was not a gentle journey, the cartwheels bumping around as they trundled over the rough roads. Back in Halliwell Thomas was put to bed but there was no rest for him. He thrashed around in great pain all night and the following morning surgeon Mr Joseph Goodwin and Dr Settle were called in. It was all to no avail. Thomas died at nine o'clock that evening.

The next day Samuel Bennett, aged seventeen, was arrested by PC Fitton. The Coroner's inquest heard that Thomas's back had been broken, and he was paralysed, and it was this which had caused his death. The jury brought in a verdict of manslaughter against Samuel and he was sent for trial at Manchester Assizes. Samuel's defence was that he had been so drunk that he didn't know what he was doing. Given Samuel's previous relationship with his father, and his dependency on him, it was obvious that he had not wilfully intended to kill him. No doubt some allowance was made for diminished responsibility and Samuel Bennett was sentenced to twelve months in prison.

CHAPTER 17

The Moors Murder
1838

It was a horribly gruesome death

T he social conscience of a Blackburn draper is more responsible for this murder becoming a classic in the annals of foul deeds in Bolton than the victim, the murderer or the method used to despatch that unfortunate person. There is also something wildly romantic about lonely moors, a celebration of the wide open spaces of beauty which can be stunning, savage and downright spooky in turn. Today, fast roads cross many tracts of moorland and travellers often don't have the time to appreciate or savour the feel, the smells, the essence of the open moors. Travellers in eighteenth and nineteenth century England regularly used the moorland tracks and pathways and old drovers roads to reach their destinations. There were many inns along the way offering hospitality, refreshment, and convivial company. They were

George Henderson was travelling from Bolton to Belmont when he was murdered.
Author's collection

places to exchange news and gossip, to tell stories and to pick up useful bits of information; a chance to socialise before the next solitary leg of the journey.

George Henderson was a young Scotsman who came from Annan in Dumfriesshire. He worked as a salesman for John Jardine, a firm of Blackburn drapers. Although he was only twenty he was successful in his job and he enjoyed travelling around from place to place. On 9 November he was on his way to Belmont for his employers. He would collect payments for orders already placed and delivered as well as taking new orders. It was the tail end of the year, a season of greyness, damp and fog which heralded the onset of winter. George didn't mind. He was in good spirits. He had already collected quite a bit of cash and he was looking forward to taking plenty of Christmas orders. There would be some good commission for him.

He decided to call in at the beer house at *Five Houses* close to Bolton before he tackled the crossing of Horwich Moor. There were a number of people drinking in the beer house and George took his beer to where a group of men were talking in front of the welcoming open fire. He stayed perhaps a little longer than he'd intended; might have drunk a little more than he'd intended; maybe said a little more than he'd intended. When he left around noon the wind was chill and put his hands in his pockets and hunched his shoulders against the cold as he set off along the moorland track which led to Winter Hill and across Horwich Moor.

The lonely drover's road across Winter Hill on which George Henderson was travelling when he was killed. The author

A few hours later George Henderson was found in a ditch alongside the track. He had been shot. The bullet '...passed through his head from his right ear and out from his left eye...' Unbelievably, he was still just alive when he was found but he died shortly after being carried back to the beer house. It was a horribly gruesome death. At first it was assumed that robbery was the motive but none of his money had been taken. His employers offered a reward, for information about his murder, of £100 (worth £5,265 today), an enormous sum which showed in what regard they had held the young man.

A twenty-two-year-old collier named William Whittle, from *Five Houses*, was eventually arrested and tried at Liverpool Assizes for the murder of George Henderson. He was acquitted however because no money had been taken from Henderson; so there was no motive and little else to connect Whittle with Henderson. Whittle admitted being in the area at the time; and he had been seen by witnesses, but there was no proof that he had killed George Henderson.

George Henderson was buried at Mount Street Chapel in Blackburn. The chapel was demolished in 1964 when its graveyard was cleared of burials, with remains being interred in Pleasington Cemetery. The headstone for Henderson's grave was lost in the move but there is a memorial to him still on Horwich Moor. After his death an oak stake was erected by John Jardine and his brother William (who had put up the reward money and paid for George's headstone) at the spot where George Henderson had been shot. It became known as the Scotchman's Stump. In 1912 it was replaced with an iron memorial in the form of part of an iron pillar from the spinning room of a cotton mill and a memorial plaque. The reason for his murder continues to remain a mystery.

★ The Winter Hill murder of George Henderson has become a local *cause célèbre* and there are various booklets and articles about it; but probably the best known is: Holding, David. *Murder in the Heather*. Friends of Smithills Hall, 1991.

CHAPTER 18

Mary Crompton's Baby
1902

*It was indeed a 'Catch 22' world for women in which
Mary Crompton lived*

In modern times it is hard to understand the desperation which drove girls like Mary Crompton. Today there is no shame attached to being an unmarried mother but in 1902 it was very different. Girls were still supposed to save themselves for marriage and their husbands. Those who did not were regarded as 'shop soiled', used goods, common, and were often shunned by friends, family and neighbours. Of course some girls indulged in illicit sex and got away with it, but for girls who 'found themselves in the family way' the disgrace was very public. In a society fond of double standards boys were encouraged to sow their wild oats, but evidently no-one gave any thought as to how they could do this if all girls were supposed to be virtuous, and what would happen to those girls who did oblige. Sons of the middle and upper classes often seduced servant girls in their own or each other's households. If the girl became pregnant she would suddenly find herself without a job and without a home. No blame was ever attached to the son in question. Birth control was not an option. Not only was it not officially available, especially to young unmarried women, but it was frowned upon since it robbed men of the chance to prove their virility. It was indeed a 'Catch-22' world for women in which Mary Crompton lived.

Mary Crompton was an ordinary Bolton lass who found herself in an extraordinarily difficult situation. She was born in Bolton in 1880 and grew up in the town. In the late summer of 1902 she gave birth to an illegitimate baby and found herself alone and practically friendless. The baby's father did not want to know and her family had practically disowned her for the shame she had brought on them. Mary could be forgiven for lamenting over the unfairness of life. As a young unmarried woman in 1902 she would not even have dared to ask for, let alone been given, help or advice on birth control. There were no tests available to prove paternity. If a man said a child was not his he was generally believed and there was nothing that could be done to disprove his assertion. The welfare state did not exist and if the girls' family cut her off her choices were stark. She could try and earn her own living or she could go into the workhouse.

Career options were still very limited for girls; especially for girls like Mary. Having a young baby to care for did not help. It was difficult for her to even rent a room when she had a child but no wedding ring. Mary was struggling but eventually she found a live-in position as a domestic servant at the *Victoria Inn* in Westhoughton close to Bolton. She managed to arrange for her child to be nursed by a lady called Ellen Lee who lived at 191 Bolton Road in Westhoughton. Ellen and her husband, William, already had children and the little bit of extra money would come in useful. Mary said that she would come and see the baby regularly.

For a while all went well and the baby thrived. Then on the evening of 11 March 1903, when the baby was about seven months old, Mary arrived at Ellen's house as usual and announced that she was taking her child to see a Mr Potter whom she was visiting. Ellen dressed the baby warmly for the evening was chilly and Mary set off into the darkness carrying the child in her arms.

It was about nine-thirty when Mary returned. Ellen noticed at once that something was wrong. The baby was crying and frothing at the mouth which appeared to be swollen and blistered. Concerned, Ellen asked Mary if she had given the baby something. Mary seemed confused and stammered that she had only given the child 'some thick Spanish' (a kind of linctus). Ellen also noticed that the baby's pinafore was missing but Mary said that the child had been sick and she had left the pinafore with Mrs Potter who had kindly offered to wash it. The smell of carbolic was very strong and Ellen discovered that the baby's frock was saturated with it. She pulled the tiny dress off the child and asked Mary again what she done, but Mary simply repeated her story and then left to return to the inn.

Ellen didn't know what to do. She gave the baby some castor oil to try and soothe the pain, then she took the child to one her friends, Mrs Margaret Halliwell, who lived up the road at number 218. Mrs Halliwell was alarmed at the state of the child and said that she should take the baby at once to see Dr Mercer. The doctor examined the baby and was shocked to discover that someone had attempted to feed the poor little mite with carbolic acid. Fortunately, he said, not enough had been given to cause the child any real lasting harm and he believed that, with treatment and care, the baby would make a full recovery.

Mary returned to Ellen's house the next day to see her child. Margaret Halliwell's husband, John, was there and he questioned Mary about what had really happened to her baby. At first Mary told the same story she had told Ellen the night before but finally she broke down and admitted that she had given the baby 'something out of a bottle'. She wouldn't say any more, but it was enough, and the police were called. Mary was arrested by Inspector Tracey and Police Constable Inniss and taken for questioning to Chequerbent police station.

The child's pinafore was retrieved from Mrs Potter and was found to have burns on it caused by carbolic acid which would have accounted for the child's frock being saturated and smelling strongly of carbolic. Mary was remanded in custody.

Questioned again she tearfully told Superintendent Leeming that life as single mother was so very hard, and people had been telling lies about her, so she had decided to 'make away with herself and her child.' She had found a bottle of carbolic acid in a cupboard at the *Victoria Inn* where she worked and saw it as a means of solving all her problems.

Mary appeared before Bolton Magistrates (JP Haslam and T Roscoe) but they did not believe her story of her intended suicide after the child's murder. Infanticide by a mother was, and still is, regarded as the most heinous of crimes. It was, also, in 1902, an offence to commit, or to even try and commit suicide. However there was a distinct lack of evidence that Mary had ever intended to harm herself. If she had really intended to kill both herself and her child with the carbolic acid she would have taken, or at least tried to take, some of it herself, and there would have been the tell tale burn marks and frothing at the mouth that her baby had suffered. Her case wasn't helped either by the fact that she had told Mrs Halliwell the day before the baby had been given the carbolic that she hoped the child would die. As far as the magistrates were concerned Mary was just looking for an easy way out of a difficult situation, and accordingly she was committed for trial at Manchester Assizes on a charge of attempted murder. Mary knew that the law would take its course and that she would never be allowed to see her child again. It was a worse punishment than anything she could ever have inflicted upon herself.

CHAPTER 19

The Gold Rush Murder
1850

*'I was horrified by seeing him lying on his back
in the middle of the river...'*

Although this murder did not take place in Bolton the victim was a Bolton man and his unusual story offers a unique insight into one of the most exciting episodes of American history. Bolton, like the rest of the Lancashire cotton towns, was heavily dependent on exports of American cotton to keep the mills working. Cotton was king in North West England during this time and Britain was approaching the zenith of her wealth and empire, but workers were paying a heavy price for the country's new found prosperity.

Edwin Moore was born in 1822, the son of Dr John Moore and his wife who lived at Hill-Cot, Sharples, in Bolton. The doctor was locally respected and earned a good if modest income. Both Edwin and his brother, Henry, were well educated and decided, encouraged by their father who wanted a good life for his sons, that emigration might offer them a better living than the grim grey smoggy millscapes of Bolton. So they planned a three year trip to see the world, and specifically to visit Van Dieman's Land to reconnoitre the Australian colonies and decide if emigration would be beneficial. On 23 August 1847 they set sail from England and arrived in Australia nearly four months later on 16 December.

Both brothers were literate and wrote frequently to their parents back home in Bolton. They spent several months exploring little known parts of Van Dieman's Land and endured many hardships, but they found the sense of adventure and exploration exhilarating. Then, as they were on the point of leaving for Port Phillip in South Australia, news of the California gold rush reached the Australian coast. Edwin and Henry quite literally saw a golden opportunity and sailed instead for San Francisco at the end of June in 1849. The voyage was a long one but they finally arrived on 29 October that year and set about making their plans.

They decided to winter in San Francisco and, together with three friends whom they had met on board ship, they built a large wattle and daub hut, on a hill about a mile out of town, as their winter base, and settled down to wait for the spring. On 14 January 1850 Edwin Moore wrote to his parents:

> *...the weather has been pretty fine during the day but wet at night, which some of the knowing say is a sign that the winter being nearly over. Should we keep our health until the summer after next and be successful at the mines, I hope we shall see you again for a short time, though I think we shall eventually settle in one of the Australian colonies. You may have many enquiries from persons wishing to come out here, I advise no one to come, though I were in England, knowing what I do now of this place, I would, from the love of adventure, chance it. It is a chance; for you may lose health which you cannot purchase with gold...*

The doctor's son seemed only too aware of the dangers offered by the New World.

Nevertheless, Edwin and Henry, together with four others, purchased a six ton long boat for 375 dollars, and sailed on 18 February 1850, heading for Yuba-ville on the way to California. They were all in good health and high spirits, looking forward to their adventure. Nothing more was heard from them, however, and Dr Moore and his wife became concerned, especially after Edwin's warnings about the health problems which they faced. Then, almost a year later, they finally received a letter from Henry written the previous October after he had spent a couple of days working in the western branch of the Feather River. The story he had to tell was a sad and macabre one which gives a unique insight into the lives of the gold prospectors and the occupational hazards that they had to face:

> *...on Wednesday morning, October 16, I got up at six o'clock and lit the fire, and not feeling well, being very much griped, I*

turned in again. I had been working in the water rather late in the evening and contributed my illness to that. Edwin cooked his breakfast, consisted of a fried cake, molasses and tea; and whilst he was eating it, a party of Indians, about five or six in number, came to the tent. They had a gun, a rifle and an old pistol. I was under no apprehension from them as they had always been very peaceable, and we have often had them working for us. Two of them had been there the day previous; I and Edwin had been on the bar by ourselves when more than a dozen had come there; they neither molested nor stole anything...

Edwin gave me a Dover's powder and told me to be still, and shortly after said he would go and "work" [supervise] the Indians... about half an hour after, I saw an Indian stealing my gun away from the tent door. I got up immediately and asked him where he was going; he said he was going to shoot much flesh... another [Indian] took his rifle which he had left by the tent, and they both made off up the hill. I followed the one who had stolen my gun and wrenched it out of his hands, but he took away my powder flask. I only had a charge of shot in my gun... I cried out for Edwin, not being able to see the spot where he was working... Receiving no answer, I went down to the place; and, finding blood on the ground, I conjectured they had thrown him into the river. I rushed in as I was, and followed it down about a quarter of a mile, hoping to be in time to save his life, if he had only been wounded... I thought I saw his hat floating down; but not finding him I turned back with feelings not to be envied...

When I got a few yards below where the blood was, I was horrified by seeing him lying on his back in the middle of the river, in about three feet of water. I rushed in and hauled him out, but he was quite dead and cold; having received five wounds on the head and chest with an axe, each of them sufficient to deprive him of life instantaneously. I laid him down on the bank; covered him up, and then made the best of my way, just as I was, with only a red shirt, red drawers, and gun, by the most scrubby road I could find to the nearest cabin, distant five miles. I did not go to the tent again, for fear the Indians might be ransacking it. When I got to the cabin I found nearly all the men sick and unable to render me any assistance, so I went five miles further and got five men to lend me a hand to bury him.

*We went down to the tent and found that the Indians had not
been there since I left, nor had they taken anything away with
them except the axe with which the deed was committed, and my
powder flask. The gold we had I could not find; but I don't think
the Indians took it, for Edwin, the night before, said he should
stow it away... We buried him, high up on the banks of the river,
and covered the grave with stones;... there may he rest in peace.
I cannot conjecture why the Indians murdered him and spared
me. He had been uniformly kind to them and to everybody else,
and was deeply regretted by all who knew him, and by none more
so than myself, who feel his loss deeply...he was as good and kind
a brother who ever lived...*

Henry went on in his letter to describe how a party of twenty-
eight men from various places, including a Mr Morley from
Bolton, whose father kept a hat shop near Market Street,
formed a posse and set out to find the killers. They attacked
one Indian camp after a volley of arrows prevented them from
having the 'parley' with the Indians that they had desired and
seven Indians were killed in the ensuing gunfire. Henry wrote:
'... two women were shot in mistake, for they all go naked, and
our men could not tell the difference...'

This is a strange thing for him to have written because they
would be the first men in history unable to tell the difference
between men and women.

Next day the self-styled posse went to attack another Indian
camp but this one was deserted. After that they seem to have
run out of steam because the posse broke up and they went
their separate ways. Henry and a man named Gatehouse tried
to recover their boat from Yuba-ville, but without success, and
eventually returned to San Francisco where Henry noted
'...fine new buildings have sprung up and streets run where
water used to flow...'

Henry Moore's letter raises almost as many questions about
the fate of Edwin Moore as it answers. As he himself said the
behaviour of the Indians is odd. Why should they leave a
potential witness alive when they outnumbered him and could
have easily killed him instead of just disarming him? What was
their motive for killing Edwin? Robbery would have been an

obvious one but Henry says they took nothing from the tent and he is fairly certain that they did not find the gold. The gold itself raises several questions. Although they had only been there two days they must have found quite an amount or why would Edwin feel the need to hide it? Moreover, the brothers seemed to be close so why did Edwin not tell Henry where he had hidden the gold? Why did they not hide it together? Why is Henry anxious to exonerate the Indians from having taken it? He felt badly enough about them for taking his brother's life.

The case was reported in the Bolton newspapers and then the historical record goes silent about Henry Moore. Did he return home to see his parents, as might be expected given the tragic circumstances he had related in his letter, or did he fulfil alone the dream he and Edwin had of settling in Australia? The Bolton Street Directories for the 1850s, 1860s and 1870s do not show a Henry Moore, but it is quite possible he returned to England though not to his home town. If Henry did survive, and he did return to England, was he still alive in the 1890s when Buffalo Bill brought his party of Indian Chiefs to nearby Manchester? How would he have felt about that? If he ever saw the pictures in the local newspapers of Buffalo Bill and his Indians riding one of the new tramcars, he must have reflected with bitter irony on the fate of his brother that autumn day in 1850 prospecting for gold in a remote Californian river.

' *I was horrified by seeing him lying on his back in the middle of the river*'.
Hannah Niblett

CHAPTER 20

Too Many Children
1835

...there was something not right about these two deaths.

L ittle William Orrell was just four-years-old and his life was already worse than that of most people. His mother had recently died and his father, John Orrell, was not long out of prison. His elder brothers and sisters had left home, if it could be called that. He could just remember a life on the farm when everything had seemed like fun. Now he had to live in a small eight feet high cellar which was close, damp, dark and unhealthy and there was no one to cuddle him when he felt frightened or sick or alone. His big sister, Elizabeth, was eight-years-old to his four and sometimes she tried to be loving to him but she'd been so ill of late and all she wanted to do was huddle in their bed and sleep.

He heard the door latch being lifted and John Orrell came into the cellar, bringing with him some bread which William knew would be for their supper. His father brewed strong dark tea and slopped some into a saucer for William to drink when it had cooled. William didn't really like tea; it was too bitter and his belly hurt every time he had it, but he drank every last drop

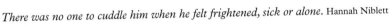

There was no one to cuddle him when he felt frightened, sick or alone. Hannah Niblett

because he knew that his father would not give him any bread until the tea saucer was empty. He missed his mother's potato pie and the lob scouse that she used to make, but his father was no cook and William knew better than to ask for more than he was given. John Orrell had a wicked temper. That night William felt worse than usual after he had drunk his tea. His belly was griping and he whimpered with the pain. Crawling onto the bed, he lay next to his sister, curled up in a tight ball to try and stop himself from being sick. It was no use. Two days later little William Orrell was dead.

On Sunday, 22 February 1835 the Orrell's neighbour, Margaret Pincock, was called out at seven in the morning to lay out the tiny pathetic body of William Orrell. She didn't like the look of his sister either. Elizabeth was thin and wan and she could not keep any food down. She looked very ill and her father really ought to get the doctor into her. Mrs Pincock shook her head. She had never liked John Orrell. William was buried on the following Tuesday at Deane Church and Mrs Pincock shed the tears for him that she knew his father wouldn't. Thirty-six hours later, at two in the morning, there was a hammering at her front door. Mrs Pincock struggled from her bed to find John Orrell standing on her doorstep once more. Her services were required again but this time it was his daughter, Elizabeth. The dead girl lay on the bed and John Orrell told Mrs Pincock that she had died of a '...sickness and relaxation of the bowels...' and Mrs Pincock was to lay her out as she had done her brother.

Child mortality was common enough in the 1830s but there was something not right about these two deaths. Acting on 'information received' Richard Daly, the Boroughreeve (chief magistrate) of Great Bolton, went to the Orrell's home together with Messrs Hamers, Burrow, Rollinson and Lee, fellow officers. The door was locked. They waited until three o'clock then sent for a man to pick the lock. Entering the cellar they found the girl's body laid out on the bed. A search of the place was made and a small paper package of arsenic was discovered hidden on top of a beam which ran across the room just below the ceiling. Orrell returned to the house at about twenty to four and was arrested at once by Rollinson and Lee. Elizabeth's body was taken away for post-mortem examination.

The post-mortem was carried out by Mr Heap. It revealed inflammation of several internal organs including the stomach, intestines and bowel. The stomach contained a great deal of dark brown fluid and a white powder which he believed to be arsenic. Watsons Chemists of Little Bolton examined this white powder and the white powder found in the package discovered in the cellar. Both proved to be arsenic. An order was made for Elizabeth's little brother, William, to be exhumed and an autopsy revealed similar symptoms of arsenic poison in his body as well as traces of the white powder.

James Horrocks, chemist and druggist of Bradshawgate, said that the writing found on the packet of arsenic in the cellar was his. He had written *Arsnic Poison* instead of *Arsenic Poison* on the label which is why he remembered this particular packet. They were busy at the time and so he had not altered it to the correct spelling. He had sold John Orrell two ounces of arsenic on 11/12 February; now only one ounce and one drachm remained. Twenty-eight grains of arsenic was enough, he said, to '...extinguish life in a few hours...'

The children's mother, who had died so suddenly just two weeks before her children, was also exhumed from the same grave but no traces of arsenic were found in her stomach. Her death, in the light of what had happened to her children, was extremely suspicious, but on-one seemed to suggest that other tests should be carried out. Her cause of death was not given in court but it must have been sudden since up to just a few weeks beforehand she had been holding her family together, visiting John Orrell in prison and taking him money. If her death was due to some kind of accident it would be even more suspicious; especially given that former fellow prisoners would later testify that he made threats against both his wife and the two youngest children.

The inquest, which was being held at the *Three Arrows*, was adjourned so that the children and their mother could be re-interred together in the family's grave at Deane Church. The burials duly took place on Monday afternoon and on the following Friday the inquest was resumed and a number of witnesses were called.

Deane church, near Bolton. The author

John Orrell, the uncle and a man of the same name as the accused, said he'd visited the cellar on the 22 February just after the boy's death and said that he thought his nephew had been looking after the children well enough. He had heard the girl asking for water although his nephew wanted to give her gin and water as he could not afford a doctor or the services of the dispensary, but the child had refused this. He was of the opinion that his nephew had 'behaved to the children as well as he could.'

A lady called Christiana Seddon had called to see John Orrell on the Wednesday, the day between the deaths of William and Elizabeth. She had discovered that the late Mrs Orrell was her second cousin. She said that Elizabeth was sick in bed and that Orrell was drinking tea. She had asked where the other children were and Orrell had replied that two were with his mother and the other two were with his uncle David. Christiana Seddon had taken her leave then but had called back later in the day. Elizabeth had still been very sick and she was begging for cold water to drink, but Orrell had refused to give her water saying that too much would make her worse. Christiana had pleaded with Orrell to call a doctor but again he had refused saying to her that the girl '...would not take good stuff [gin and water] and was therefore unlikely to take physic...' Elizabeth was in a pitiful state and kept crying 'oh my belly!' Christiana had examined the child's belly and said that '...it is almost clung to its back...'

Selina Norris of Heaton (her husband and Mrs Orrell were brother and sister) also gave evidence. Orrell's eldest daughter, Sarah, was staying with her. Selina said that she had called at the house on Monday, 23 February and while she was there Elizabeth had drunk some tea from a saucer and was then violently sick. However she had seen her take some toast while her father ate bread and butter. She said that Elizabeth had been a healthy enough child although she had suffered from smallpox.

Sarah Orrell, Orrell's eldest daughter was sixteen. She said that when Orrell was released from prison in the January the family were living at Barrow Bridge near Bolton. Her mother had died on 4 February that year and her father moved to Bolton with the two youngest children, Elizabeth and William. Sarah had at first lived with her grandmother before going to stay with Selina. She said that she visited Bolton on Sunday, 22 February and saw her brother dead in the cradle. Elizabeth was very ill. She had been sick twice and purged twice while Sarah

Graveyard at Deane church where William and Elizabeth Orrell lie buried with their mother. The author

was there. Her father told her that William had appeared to be well since they went to Bolton and he showed Sarah what he said was a bottle of godfrey which he'd given to William when he became ill.

John Orrell had been a farmer but he had fallen on hard times. He had come to Bolton seeking work but had not been able to find a job in the town. He desperately wanted to go to America and make a fresh start but he was told that he could not do so on his own with the two young children. On 10 February he rented cellar accommodation in Commission Street, Bolton Moor. Thomas Young, a servant of the landlord, had swept out the cellar prior to Orrell's arrival. The parcel of arsenic had been hidden on a beam which ran across the ceiling about eight feet from the ground. A child could not have reached it. Young insisted he'd swept the beam as well because the cellar had been unoccupied from 12 November to 10 February before Orrell took possession.

On 21 January 1834 John Orrell had been sent to Lancaster prison for debt and had been discharged on 7 January 1835. He had a reputation as a man of violent temper. When he was in prison he had been put in a cell by himself. While there he was often heard to declare that he would murder his wife and children when he was released; usually after his wife had visited and failed to bring him sufficient funds. He often said that the two youngest children were not his and was always in 'a passion' when he spoke of his wife and these two children. This accusation was never investigated although it might have had an important bearing on the case. It may just have been the overworked imagination of a jealous and violent man forcibly detained while his wife had her liberty, but he certainly came to believe it with tragic consequences.

The Coroner's jury found John Orrell guilty of murder and he was committed for trial at Lancaster Assizes. Orrell pleaded insanity and said that when he'd been in prison for debt he had often thought he was God and the prison surgeon had noted that he suffered from delusions. The jury disagreed and took just five minutes to find him guilty and he was sentenced to death. Orrell showed no remorse and declared his innocence to the end.

CHAPTER 21

Hall i' th' Wood
1784-1790

...ruined by the greedy 'con-merchants'

A romantic black and white timbered Tudor mansion hidden from view among a forest of oak trees with a tinkling brook flowing through the meadows below sounds like the stuff of fairy tales; not the sort of setting where a family would cower in fear as men climbed the outside of the house, intent on spying within, and ominous sounds came from the darkened attics.

Hall i' th' Wood (pronounced halliwood) stands above Eagley Brook on the outskirts of present-day Bolton. As its name suggests it once stood in the middle of a wood. There is little trace of that now. The Hall is partially surrounded by a modern housing estate and the sweeping meadow in front of the Hall is

Hall i' th' Wood, home of Samuel Crompton. The author

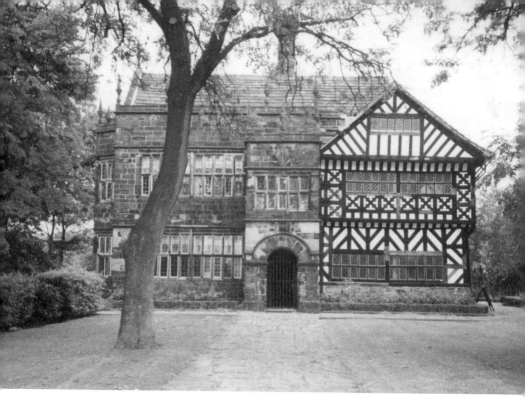

Hall i' th' Wood, the room where Crompton worked on his mule is on the first floor, to the left of the front door. The author

bounded by a fast road and a small industrial estate. Hall i' th' Wood still has the power to fascinate those who step inside. As the door closes behind visitors, they are transported back to the time when the most monstrous foul deeds robbed a man of his home, his invention, his livelihood, and, ultimately, his life.

Samuel Crompton was born in 1753, the son of George and Elizabeth Crompton, at Firwood Fold Farm close to Hall i' th' Wood. He was five when the family moved to Hall i' th' Wood. Samuel attended a school on Church Street in Bolton, not far from the barber's shop on Churchgate owned by Richard Arkwright, the supposed inventor of the water frame. Samuel's father died while he was still quite young, but he continued to live at the Hall with his mother, two younger sisters, and his disabled uncle, Alexander Crompton.

In his early twenties, irritated by the limitations of the spinning jenny which he and his mother used to spin yarn for him to weave, he set about trying to invent a machine which would spin yarn faster. He worked in an upstairs room at the

Hall which was not used by the family and which had plenty of light. There were set-backs and frustrations and when it all got too much, Samuel, an accomplished musician who sometimes played with the Bolton orchestra, would sit and play his fiddle while he calmed himself down enough to begin work again. Eventually he produced the spinning mule, so called because a mule is part horse and part donkey and this machine was a combination of Arkwright's water frame and Hargreaves' spinning jenny. The mule produced consistent good quality fine yarn which was especially suitable for weaving muslins.

However, in 1779 there were riots in Bolton and other towns when much of what was termed 'the new fangled machinery' was destroyed by those who believed that this mechanisation was costing them their jobs. Samuel was afraid. His invention had taken years of effort and he did not want it smashed in a few moments of madness by an ignorant mob. Hall i' th' Wood had an extensive roof space which gave Samuel an idea. He climbed up and took a look round. There was some planking across the joists and a small window which gave a little light. The roof was sloping and he could barely stand upright but he realised that this large dimly lit attic would be ideal for his purpose. Scrambling back down he carefully dismantled his mule into movable sections and took each one up into the attic. In a small area close to the window so that he could see what he was doing he removed some planking and a few cross struts until he had created a space similar to a large unshaped coffin. Into this space he carefully packed all his machine parts and then recovered them with the planking. It was perfect. They

The plaque above the newsagent's shop on Deansgate marks the site of Richard Arkwright's barber shop, 1760-68. The author

could look but no-one would realise that there was anything there.

His plan succeeded. After the disturbances were over he reassembled his mule and began to spin with it again. He earned good money for his yarn and in 1780, buoyed up by his new found affluence, he married Mary Pimlott, a weaver from the nearby village of Turton, at Bolton Parish Church. They settled at Hall i' th' Wood and started their family. His son, George, was born in 1781. However there was gossip in the town about his new invention and ever increasing numbers of dealers began coming to Hall i' th' Wood to buy his yarn but also to try and find out how he could produce such consistent quality in such consistent quantity. When he refused to tell them matters took a sinister turn.

Day and night Samuel and his family found themselves besieged. There were people in their garden; people peering through their downstairs windows; people climbing their walls looking through their upstairs windows; would-be industrial spies trying to get a sight of his machine. Mary, his mother and sisters, and his young son were thoroughly frightened by the faces at the windows. Samuel, concerned and angry, dismantled his machine again and removed it to the attic. This time he didn't hide it but tried to work up there away from all the prying eyes. It was impossible in that dark cramped space. He realised that he could no longer keep the mule a secret.

Samuel couldn't afford to patent the mule so it was suggested to him by Bolton cotton merchant, John Pilkington, that all the textile manufacturers should contribute to a subscription list and in return Samuel would make his spinning mule openly available. This sounded a good idea but Samuel was no businessman. Once the machine was on the market the list and subscription amounts dwindled dramatically and he made just £60 (worth around £4,800 today) for an invention which revolutionised the burgeoning cotton industry. It was not enough. Reluctantly he decided to leave Hall i' th' Wood.

The Crompton family moved first to Oldhams Farm in the nearby village of Sharples, and then, in 1791, to King Street in Bolton. While the cotton manufacturers prospered and fortunes were made, Samuel struggled to make a living as a hand loom weaver, an occupation which was now fast becoming obsolete, and sank into debt. The stress took its toll on his family and Mary died in 1796 leaving him with eight young children to care for. Samuel spent the rest of his life trying to gain appropriate recognition for his invention until finally, his health destroyed, he died in 1827, bitter, disillusioned and impoverished, at his house in King Street.

Samuel's hiding place for his spinning mule in the attic at Hall i' th' Wood is still there but it is not on public view for health and safety reasons. His house in King Street no longer exists; the present street consisting simply of a large car park and one wall of the Post Office. His children and their descendants are scattered. His invention, which revolutionised the cotton industry and made so many people rich, is just a page in the history books. His life, once so promising but ruined by the greedy 'con-merchants' prepared to stop at nothing, is almost forgotten. In 1862 a statue to Samuel Crompton's memory was finally erected by the people of Bolton. It was far too little far too late.

Below: Samuel Crompton's tomb in St Peter's parish churchyard. The author

Inset: Statue of Samuel Crompton, Nelson Square, off Bradshawgate. The author

CHAPTER **22**

Sarah McClelland
1830

She was lying on her back, her eyes wide open...
almost naked from the waist down.

It was growing dusk and the old lady shivered and pulled her red cloak tighter around herself to keep out the bitter cold. Lord, but she was tired. It seemed a long time since she had left her Bolton fireside to walk to her daughter's house. Oldham couldn't be far now. She would not normally make the journey at this time of year but it was nearly Christmas and what with the baby coming she knew her daughter would welcome her being there. She felt lonely now that nice young weaver to whom she'd been chatting had bid her farewell and turned off her road for his own house. Silently and wearily she trudged along, keeping a steady pace.

The lights of a beer house shone dully in front of her. She had no money for beer, though the Lord knew she could do with a glass of something to warm her. Her mouth was dry and she was thirsty. Serve her right for talking to everyone she met along the road. She tapped timidly on the back door of the beer house which proclaimed itself to be *Moor's Beer House*. The woman who answered the door seemed pleasant

Sarah McClelland glanced nervously over her shoulder: was that a noise?
Hannah Niblett

enough and the old lady hesitantly asked if she might have some water to drink. To her unending gratitude the woman let her stand before the kitchen range to warm herself while she drank her water. They didn't talk much as the woman was busy and helping to serve in the bar, but she smiled and offered her hostess the season's greetings as she took her leave.

Outside it was quite dark but there was a bit of a moon. She walked slowly along the old track. Straight as a dye it was. Lonely too. Not many houses out this way. An owl hooted close by and startled her. She turned. Was that a noise she heard. No, it wasn't coming from behind her; it was coming from somewhere in front of her. She strained her eyes into the darkness, a little afraid now. What was it that she couldn't see but she which she sensed was there? Cautiously she stepped forward then she opened her mouth and screamed.

It was two days before Christmas and the lad on his way to work at Ashton's warehouse in Newton Heath was thinking of how he would spend his precious day off on Christmas Day. Church in the morning of course, and this year they would have a goose for their Christmas dinner so there was great excitement. His father had won it in a raffle at the *Three Crows*. Then in the evening perhaps he could visit Lizzie's family. He was walking along a lonely part of the Roman Road that was called Street at Cutler's Hill in Hollinwood. Lost in his daydreaming he didn't notice the body until he almost fell over it. Startled, he stepped back and gasped in horror. There at his feet lay a woman. She was lying on her back, her eyes wide open, and she was almost naked from the waist down.

Thoroughly frightened, he set off at a run. The first person he met was a local man named Jonas Schofield. Close to tears now he blurted out what he'd found. Jonas patted his shoulder reassuringly and told the lad to leave matters to him. Jonas Schofield was as good as his word. He enlisted some help from a few local men and set off up the old Roman road. The woman was lying there just as the lad had described her. Jonas was shocked. She was no longer young and she looked pathetic lying there, her worn flesh exposed to the elements, robbing of her dignity. He bent down and gently closed her eyes, noticing as he did so that her grey hair was frozen to the ground. There were footmarks on the ground nearby and her bonnet and cap lay some distance away. It was a bad business he thought.

They moved the woman's body to Mr Barrow's at the *Wheatsheaf* public house and an inquest was held there on Christmas Eve. The local surgeon said that she had suffered a fit and then died of exposure and the Coroner's jury recorded a verdict of death by natural causes. Jonas Schofield protested violently. This was no natural death. She had been attacked, raped and murdered, he was sure of it. It was no use. The Coroner supported his jury's verdict. One problem remained however. She was a stranger to those parts and the Coroner wanted an identification before her body was released for burial.

Sitting in the public seats was the wife of a local weaver, Robert Lees, from Watch Cote in Failsworth. Over their dinner that night she told her husband about the excitement at the Coroner's court. Robert looked thoughtful. Two nights ago, on the 22 December, as he was returning from his work in Manchester, he had overtaken an elderly woman. They had walked together for a short while, chatting together companionably. She had said that she was very tired. She'd left her home in Bolton that afternoon and was going to visit her daughter who lived in Oldham with her husband, a mechanic at Cousins' factory there. When they had reached Robert's turning he bid her goodnight and they went their separate ways.

Robert went at once to the local constable and told him what he knew. The constable made enquiries. It did not take long. The dead woman was identified by her daughter as Sarah McClelland. Sarah was the wife of a weaver and lived at Howell Croft in Bolton. She was sixty-seven years of age and she had had fourteen children of whom seven were still living. She had lost seven of her children and then she had lost her life in a terrible manner. Although they had not known her in life, Robert and Jonas and many others in the parish felt grief for her and some sort of collective responsibility for the dreadful way in which she had died. Now that she had been identified Sarah McClelland was laid to rest in Newton Heath Parish Church.

Howell's Court (frontages) today. The author

That might have been the end of the story but it wasn't. The following month, January 1831, rumours began to surface that Jonas Schofield had been closer to the truth than he knew when he said that she had not died a natural death, that she had been murdered. Mr Ashton, the Hollinwood constable, made enquiries. Meanwhile news eventually reached Jonas Schofield's ears that one of his wife's friends, a lady named Mrs Mellor, was sporting a new red cloak given to her by her husband. Jonas knew her husband, John Mellor, who was a collier, and knew that he did not earn enough money to buy his wife any new clothes. Jonas remembered that Sarah McClelland's cloak had never been found. It had puzzled him at the time that she had not been wearing any outer garments to protect her against the bitter cold, but Robert Lees had been adamant that when he had walked along the road with her that December night she had been muffled up in a distinctive long red cloak.

Jonas went straight to Mr Taylor, the constable of Failsworth. Together Mr Taylor and Mr Ashton went to John Mellor's house and searched it. Lying on the bed they found a cloak which matched the description of the cloak Sarah McClelland had been wearing. Mrs Mellor said her husband had returned home at about eleven o'clock on the 22 December and had given her the cloak which he said he had found lying on the roadway. John Mellor was arrested. Mellor protested his innocence. He had been on his way home along a footpath by the canal leading to the Old Road between Manchester and Oldham at around ten thirty on the night in question when he met Ashton Worrall who had asked him to take the cloak home and to say nothing about where he had got it.

Ashton Worrall, aged twenty-five, and his brother William, who was thirty-eight-years-old, were well known in the district. Ashton kept a horse and cart and acted as a carrier while his brother William cut hay for local farmers. William's wife was a weaver in a nearby mill. The Worrall brothers were then arrested. They too protested their innocence and said they had spent the evening drinking with Ashton Hilton, a seventeen-year-old youth who was a servant to various local carters and farmers and had done carting work for Ashton Worrall. Hilton was also arrested and questioned, like the others, by Mr Holme, the magistrate. Ashton Hilton was younger and less worldly wise than the Worralls; and he was scared. Under the intense questioning he broke down and said he would tell all that he knew. It was a sordid tale which emerged.

He had spent the evening with the Worrall brothers at the *Sun Inn* which was owned by Mrs Lane, the sister of Ashton and William Worrall. They left just after ten and started to make their way home to Fletcher Fold along the usual footpath across the fields. They came to a pit in a field which adjoined the Old Road and there they met a woman. Ashton Worrall began '...to pull her about...' and she struggled fiercely. Hilton went behind a bush to relieve himself and when he returned William Worrall was holding the woman down while Ashton Worrall raped her. By this time a man whom he believed to be Richard Chadderton, from his voice and dress, had arrived on the scene. According to Hilton, he and William Worrall then raped the woman in turn while Ashton Worrall held her down. While Hilton said that he didn't touch her, he also admitted that he had done nothing to help her. The men then grabbed her cloak and they all ran off over the canal bridge and down a footpath where they met John Mellor. Ashton Worrall gave him the cloak and they then retraced their steps back over the bridge and along the towpath to Fletcher Fold. Hilton stopped the night with the Worralls while Richard Chadderton made his way back to his own home in Dark Lane near Woodhouses.

Ashton and William Worrall and Richard Chadderton were indicted for the wilful murder of Sarah McClelland. At the trial (from which women were excluded on the grounds that the salacious details were altogether too dreadful for their delicate ears and constitutions) the last pitiful hours of Sarah's life were pieced together. She had met a man named Thomas Jones earlier in the evening about a hundred yards from the *Three Crows* in Newton Heath. She told him where she had come from and that she thought she had come too far. After Sarah and Robert Lees had parted company, she stopped at a beer shop owned by Samuel Moors near the canal bridge in Failsworth, about a quarter of a mile from the *Sun Inn*. She asked for a drink of water and Mrs Moors had given her one, noting her features and her unusual red cloak. Then she had stepped out into the night to continue her journey along the Old Road.

Her death had been caused by apoplexy, brought on by the shock of the rapes, and exposure. She had put up a terrific struggle for her honour and her life but she was no match for three younger men. The constable said that there had been a severe hoar frost with a sprinkling of snow and hail that night so that initially the footsteps and the trampled vegetation were not visible. This was the reason why they did not at first realise that she had been attacked, hence the original coroner's verdict. Jonas Schofield wisely kept his own counsel when he heard this. The judge pronounced that there was no real case against Chadderton since the only evidence was hearsay from a youth who thought he recognised him and the story of him suddenly coming upon the scene and just joining in may have sounded a little unlikely. Ashton and William Worrall were sentenced to death leaving Ashton Worrall's pretty wife absolutely distraught. The brothers protested their innocence to the end but the law took its course and they were executed towards the end of March in 1830.

CHAPTER 23

Shocking Murder of an Irish Navvy
1867

John McDermott lay on the floor in a pool of blood

his story has several comical elements, and had it not ended in tragedy it would have been quite amusing, but death is no laughing matter.

Bernard Comaford kept a lodging house at Albert Place, New Bury in Farnworth near Bolton. His tenants were Irish navvies who were working on the building of a new branch line which would run from Eccles to Little Hulton. Around half a dozen Irishmen were lodging with him in March 1867. Their names were: Michael Redmonds, Michael Burke, Paul James Bannan, James Power, Hugh Smith, and John McDermott who was forty-four and unmarried.

One Sunday night around the middle of March 1867 Bernard Comaford went out drinking as usual. When he finally returned home at one in the morning he found Michael Redmonds, Paul Bannan and John McDermott drunk and stretched out asleep on the living room floor. This annoyed him. He shook McDermott and Redmonds roughly by the shoulders and told them to leave his house by the following day. John McDermott opened a bleary eye and told his landlord where to go and what to do with himself. Comaford was incensed. He dragged McDermott to his feet and blows were exchanged. This disturbance woke Michael Redmonds in time to see his friend John McDermott fall to the floor and receive a savage kicking from Bernard Comaford.

Redmonds jumped up and got between McDermott and Comaford, but he was kicked several times on the thighs by Comaford, and the two of them struggled together until they fell into the street. Redmonds fell down but picked himself up and another scuffle ensued as they returned to the house. Comaford yelled angrily for his wife to bring him his knife; but unbeknown to him Mrs Comaford had fled terrified to their bedroom and hidden herself underneath the bed. As they entered the living room once more Comaford got hold of Redmonds's right hand and bit his finger and thumb. Redmonds squealed in pain. This noise woke Bannan who jumped from the floor and struck Comaford several times in the face. Comaford rushed into the kitchen, grabbed a brush handle and struck Bannan hard, knocking him out.

Redmonds, now thoroughly alarmed and in some pain, escaped from the house. Comaford yelled at him that if he showed his face again he'd knock his brains out. Through the grimy window Redmonds saw Comaford go over to McDermott's prone body and beat him with the brush handle. Redmonds tried hard to get assistance from some passers-by, but they, thinking it just a drunken Irish brawl, shrugged off his pleas for help. Desperate by now he ran to the local police station.

When the police arrived, Comaford's passion and anger seemed to be spent. He was lying on a bed asleep by the side of McDermott who was in a sitting posture on the floor with his back against the wall. He also seemed to be asleep. Redmonds tried to lift him and to speak to him but he just fell sideways onto the floor. Bannan was still flat on his back on the floor. Everything was quiet and the police took the view that they were all sleeping it off and left.

By five o'clock the police were called back to the house. John McDermott lay dead on the floor in a pool of blood. His chest, throat and face were covered in large purple bruises. A mallet, normally used to latch the front door, was discovered bloodstained and hidden behind a stone flag against the kitchen wall. The brush handle was found broken into three pieces. Mrs Comaford was still cowering terrified under the bed. Bernard Comaford was arrested.

The Coroner's Court and the inquest were held, appropriately enough, at the *Vitriol Makers Arms*, the home of Mrs Ellen Bowden, and the court room was packed. The Coroner's jury could not decide among themselves whether Bernard Comaford was guilty of a manslaughter charge or not and so he was committed for trial.

The trial took place on 10 August that same year. Mr Torr and Mr Addison for the prosecution laid out the facts of the case. Mr Cottingham, acting for the defence of Bernard Comaford, tried to blame Bannan and Redmond for the whole debacle. Bannan said he had slept through the whole thing and had heard nothing. Asked about the bloodstained mallet, Comaford claimed that it was his own blood. The judge and jury were not impressed and found Bernard Comaford guilty of manslaughter; although the judge said he accepted that Comaford may not have realised that John McDermott had been fatally injured by the blows he received. Still protesting his innocence, Bernard Comaford was sentenced to eight months in prison with hard labour.

CHAPTER 24

Suffer the Little Children
1831

1. Ellen Boardman

Her hands were bloody and there were marks and bruises on the baby and a livid appearance about the neck.

Caught in the act, one might think, reading the above description but things are not always what they seem.

Jane Boardman, who was forty-six, lived with her husband, William, and unmarried daughter, Ellen aged twenty-two, in a small cottage at Little Bolton. Much to Jane's distress, Ellen had got herself pregnant. The father was a local lad called James Slack but he could not afford to marry Ellen. However, Jane and her husband stood by their daughter and agreed that she and the baby could live them. How they would manage Jane didn't know. Money was short enough as it was.

On the morning of 29 April 1831 Ellen went into labour. Alice Berwick, a mother of four herself, was the midwife, and several neighbours came to help including Janet Austin, Sarah Halliwell, Jane Ward and her daughter, Sarah. Ellen's father was sent out for the day. Jane Ward said that it was an easy labour and Ellen's baby was born at eleven thirty according to Janet Austin. The baby was a fine healthy boy. Ellen named him James after his father. Both mother and child were put to bed and appeared to be doing well; but by five o'clock that afternoon the baby was dead and his mother was dying. Jane

Her hands were bloody and there were marks and bruises on the baby. Hannah Niblett

Boardman's hands were bloody and there were marks and bruises on the baby and a livid appearance about the neck.

Jane Boardman was arrested and indicted at Bolton-le-Moors for the murder of her grandson, James Boardman, aged one day. There was great amazement and great excitement in Bolton over this case. Ellen and her baby were buried together on Sunday 3 May at St Peter's church in Great Bolton. Large crowds turned out to the funeral. James Slack was grief-stricken, but Ellen's father, William, was utterly distraught and had to be restrained from throwing himself into the grave beside his dead daughter. Jane Boardman was not allowed to attend her daughter's funeral and she was absolutely heartbroken.

At the Coroner's inquest the details which emerged of what had happened were confused and circumstantial. At first the baby had been put into his own cot but between one and two o'clock Jane took him into bed with her. She said that Ellen was exhausted and needed to sleep but James was crying for attention so she picked him up and cuddled him. He quietened down and she took him into bed with her for she too was tired, having been up since the early hours.

Alice Berwick said that she had fed the child with some butter and sugar at around one o'clock. He had struggled so much that she was afraid he was having a fit and she had called

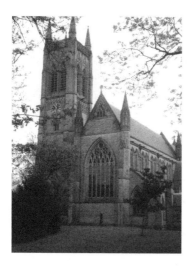

the local priest in to baptise James just in case. James obviously recovered after a cuddle and a rest with his grandmother because at three-thirty Sarah Halliwell gave him some rice tea. She said that there were no marks on his face when she did this. Afterwards she gave him to Ellen to cuddle and James remained with his

St Peter's church and churchyard, Bolton, where Mary Hopkinson and Ellen Boardman are buried. The author

mother until about four-twenty. By four-forty-five Jane Ward had returned and she and Sarah Halliwell gave Ellen some peppermint tea.

At around five o'clock Jane decided to give her daughter a gill of beer. She handed the baby to Ellen, somewhat roughly, according to the witnesses. In fact, they claimed, she had been handling the child roughly all day, and they suspected that she had also been drinking. James was not crying or protesting at this rough treatment and, concerned, the women examined him. He was dead. Ellen showed little emotion at this news but it is doubtful if she really understood what had happened. She was extremely weak and bleeding heavily. Within three quarters of an hour she too was dead.

At the Coroner's inquest, George Wostenholme, a surgeon of Little Bolton, was called to give evidence on how the mother and child had died. He said that the baby was full term and healthy. His heart was fine and his lungs were inflated showing that he had certainly been alive for a time. There was no sign of poison in his stomach. There were pinch marks on either side of the baby's face and the back of his head was swollen which seemed excessive bruising for an easy labour and a natural birth. The bruises were of externally inflicted violence but he said that they could have been caused by the midwife trying to hasten the birth and he couldn't say if they were inflicted before or after birth.

Ellen had died of blood loss. She had lost a lot of blood during labour and been very pallid afterwards. The afterbirth had not been removed because Ellen had been haemorrhaging so much that the midwife said she had mistaken that for the afterbirth. During the afternoon she had continued to bleed heavily, becoming weaker and weaker, until eventually she bled to death; her condition exacerbated by the fact that the afterbirth was still in situ.

The remaining witnesses gave slightly conflicting accounts of what had happened but they all seemed keen to blame Jane. This could have been due to the fact that there were grievances between the women before the birth (in which case why did they agree to attend?) or, as is much more likely, to cover up their own incompetence and mistakes. A woman who has had four children herself, and delivered several more, would be unlikely to mistake heavy bleeding for an afterbirth. If, as was said, the labour was easy, why was there so much blood loss? Should this not have caused concern to the midwife? Did she panic and try to forcibly drag the baby into the world?

Why was James not given to his mother for her to feed him? If she was unable to do so, and there was no other woman able to nurse him, the general practice would have been to soak a clean rag in milk or water and let the baby suck on that. Feeding a new-born butter, sugar and rice tea seems extraordinary and would horrify modern doctors. James may well have had an allergy to dairy products, hence his fierce struggles which prompted Alice to think he was having a fit. Could his 'bruising' and redness about the neck have been the results of an allergic reaction? Or maybe he was just accidentally suffocated by an exhausted adult falling asleep while cuddling him; a tragic event which sadly still happens today.

The Coroner was uneasy about the recounted details as well, although he did not have the benefit of modern medical hindsight. In the light of the medical evidence given by the surgeon, the Coroner decided that the rest of the evidence was merely circumstantial. If her daughter was bleeding to death it was unsurprising that Jane should have blood on her hands. If the baby had been roughly handled at birth it could have caused problems; but the midwife would not have wanted her reputation sullied. If, under all the circumstances, Jane had taken a drink, who could blame her? Who would not do the same in such a situation? The Coroner therefore acquitted Jane because medical evidence suggested that the marks on the baby could have been inflicted before or during birth; and because the rest of the evidence was merely circumstantial.

Jane Boardman disappeared into history. She had lost her daughter and her grandson; and her family life must have been destroyed by these events for they would probably always wonder whether she really had got away with murder or whether she had simply been a victim of rough justice?

2. Charlotte Gray

A small bundle was floating near the water's edge.

On Sunday, 20 February 1831 a young couple were 'walking out together' and their path took them through Bull's Field and Taylor's Field in Bolton where the reservoir lay which supplied the cotton mill belonging to Messrs Ormerod and Hardcastle. As they approached the dull sheet of water the girl suddenly clutched at her boyfriend's arm and pointed. A small bundle was floating near the edge. The lad found a dead branch and used it to drag the little bundle ashore. They looked at each and then nervously began to unwrap the dirty sheet tied around it. As they spread the sheet flat they looked at each other in horror. There lying on the ground before them was a tiny dead baby girl.

An inquest was held at the *Three Arrows* public house where it was established that 'the body of a fine full-grown infant' contained in the bundle was that of a female child who had been born alive. She showed signs of violent injury to the skull; an injury which, in medical opinion, was inflicted soon after her birth. It was thought that she had been dead for a just a few days. People shook their heads in sorrow. How could someone do that to a small defenceless baby? Sadly, in the nineteenth century it was not uncommon for a desperate mother to kill her new-born child because she simply could not afford to feed another mouth or because, as an unmarried mother, she could not face the shame or the hardship of bringing up a child alone. A verdict of wilful murder by person or persons unknown was brought in by the Coroner's jury.

About a week later a twenty-four-year-old local girl named Charlotte Gray was arrested. She lived in Middle Street in Bolton and was known to have been recently very heavily pregnant though there was no sign of a baby. Charlotte was unmarried but she admitted to having been expecting a baby in February. She said that she had given birth to a still-born child, a little girl, in mid February, and she had been so upset that she had thrown the child out of her bedroom window! Dr Watson examined Charlotte and said that she had indeed recently given birth. The baby had obviously been murdered but he could not prove that it was she who had killed the child. In default of bail she was committed for trial charged with concealing a birth.

At the trial little hard evidence could be offered but Charlotte was indicted for secretly disposing of her illegitimate baby girl and trying to conceal her birth. It was finally established that the child had been born and died on 15 February and that the baby girl subsequently found in the reservoir belonging to Messrs Ormerod and Hardcastle had been that born to Charlotte Gray. However, it could not be proved that Charlotte had murdered her baby. She was found guilty of concealing a birth and sentenced to two years imprisonment at Lancaster Castle, but the trial Judge said that in his opinion she was probably guilty of a much higher crime. Charlotte's small daughter was buried in an anonymous pauper's grave alone, unloved and unwanted. She never even had a name.

3. Amelia Green
...all she wanted to do was die.

This story illustrates well the harshness, and often hopelessness, of life for mill workers in nineteenth century Bolton, as well as the social climate of the times. It is also however a story that is as old as the hills. Wife left alone for months and years on end, grows bored and lonely, finds another man, moves in with him and incurs his mother's everlasting disapproval...

Amelia Green was the wife of soldier George Green who was serving in the Indies. She was however, his wife in name only since, bored and lonely on her own, she set up home with Richard Dewhurst, a stripper and grinder, who lived in a cellar on Great Moor Street in Bolton. Richard was the son of Hannah Isherwood who was aged sixty two at the time of this story. Hannah was not best pleased with Richard's domestic arrangements and she made it clear that she neither liked nor approved of Amelia. The couple ignored her obvious disapproval as best they could. They had two children together and by November 1860 Amelia was heavily pregnant with her third child.

Great Moor Street, where Amelia Green and her family lived in a cellar.
The author

On the night of 10 November, which was a Saturday, Richard, Amelia and Hannah had been out to the local pub. Amelia had not touched alcohol because of her baby but Richard and his mother had not stinted themselves. Hannah was drunk and Richard was not entirely sober. They returned home shortly after ten-thirty. Betty Taylor, the wife of the fishmonger in nearby Dawes Street, James Taylor, was in the house minding the two older children. Amelia and Hannah began quarrelling almost as soon as they got home; hurling insults and calling each other names in front of Richard, Betty and the children. Hannah lost her temper completely and became incensed with rage. She seized Amelia and pulled her down on the floor, grabbing her hair and as she did so, striking

Amelia's head against the bars that projected from the fireplace on which they put the kettle.

Blood streamed from a nasty inch long wound to the left-hand side of Amelia's head at the back. Amelia's son ran to fetch James Lee, the clock and watchmaker who lived in the shop above the cellar, sobbing that his mother was hurt. When James came down to the cellar, blood was still pouring from the wound to Amelia's head and the hearth was covered in blood. Hannah was kneeling on the floor at Richard's feet, clutching at his trousers, drunkenly pleading with him '...she has not three months to go and she'll lay this to thy charge too.' When she saw Lee standing there she began cursing and swearing and, disgusted, Lee threw her out into the street.

Betty, who left the house at around eleven-fifteen, thought that Amelia had lost nearly a pint of blood. Amelia was sitting in a chair holding a hand to her injured head and quarrelling with Richard about his mother's attack on her. When Betty saw Amelia the next afternoon, Amelia said she felt poorly. Betty washed the head wound and put a plaister on it. Amelia said her head still felt sore but it had at least stopped bleeding. She and Richard had made up their quarrel and were sitting together amicably enough. Betty made her farewells and left.

However, at four o'clock the following morning she was woken by Richard frantically knocking on her door. He asked her to come quickly as Amelia's head wound was bleeding profusely: 'running like a spigot' as he put it. Betty rushed round to Amelia's house but she couldn't stem the bleeding and she sent for James Forbes, assistant to the local surgeon, Mr Rothwell. Forbes stayed until about six. Amelia, who had lost a lot of blood, was now very weak and poorly and stayed in bed. On Tuesday afternoon, 13 November, Amelia complained of the pain and Dr Livy came to the house again. He had last seen her five days before, on the Thursday preceding Hannah's attack on her, when she complained of a pain in her side and he thought she had begun to show signs of labour although she was only six months pregnant.

Dr Livy was concerned about her and gave her something to try and ease the pain. The following day she developed a deep red skin inflammation on the left-hand side of her face.

Although she recovered within a few days her strength was failing and she was sinking gradually; saying that all she wanted to do was die.

Late in the evening of Thursday, 21 November she went into premature labour. Dr Livy returned to the house at once and at ten o'clock on Friday morning, the 22 November, Amelia was delivered of a still born infant. The doctor was by now seriously worried about her condition and he gently fed her a tablespoon of brandy and water every hour. By three o'clock she refused to take any more. She couldn't eat or drink because she found it difficult to swallow properly and she said again that she just wanted to die. That evening Amelia was finally granted her wish and slipped away quietly, despite the best efforts of Dr Livy.

The doctor said that her wound, though not initially fatal, turned out to be because she had not received proper immediate medical attention. The wound had caused the inflammation on her skin. She was not strong because she worked in a cotton mill as a drawing-frame tenter and her diet was poor and inadequate; and she took nothing to support her while she was ill. Amelia lived in 'a wretched place', a cellar 'unclean and not fit for residence' where there was much drinking and callousness. The lack of treatment for her injury, loss of blood, and shock, brought on her miscarriage; and her body just couldn't take any more.

Although the Coroner believed that Hannah had meant to give Amelia a 'good lugging' he did not believe that she had intended to kill her. Nevertheless, as a result of her drunken actions Amelia had been injured and had died as a result of that injury. A verdict and charge of manslaughter against Hannah was brought in by the jury and she was sent to await trial at Liverpool Assizes. With hindsight, however, it is probably fairer to say that Amelia's life was so wretched that she just gave up; and who could blame her? Her two young children were left motherless with a father who drank and a grandmother who hated them. Their fate is not recorded but it is probably fair to say that they would have been condemned to wretched lives if they survived.

CHAPTER 25

The Cab Murder
1889

Fletcher's eyes were open but he appeared
to be deeply unconscious.

One of the strangest episodes in the annals of Bolton foul deeds is the murder of John Fletcher, the senior partner in Robert Fletcher and Son whose paper manufacturing mills stood at Kearsley and Stoneclough just outside Bolton. The firm also had a warehouse and offices in New Cannon Street in Manchester from which much of their business and administration was conducted. John Fletcher, aged forty nine, was a widower who had no children. He was a well respected man of some importance in the Bolton area and a local County Councillor, and he visited Manchester frequently in the course of his work. On Tuesday, 26 February 1889 he went in to the Manchester offices of his company and worked at his desk until lunchtime. He seemed to be in good spirits. He left the company offices for lunch at one o'clock but he did not return afterwards and he was not seen alive again by his colleagues.

When John Fletcher left the offices he told his associates that he intended to attend a sale of mill premises which was due to take place at five o'clock in the *Mitre Hotel* at Cathedral Gates. He met an old friend from Oldham for lunch and when they parted during the course of the afternoon he reiterated his intention of attending the sale. It was arranged that he and his friend should meet up again at seven o'clock that evening after the sale. His friend waited until eight o'clock but John Fletcher did not arrive. At the time that he should have been meeting his friend, John Fletcher and a respectably dressed young man of about twenty years old engaged Henry Golding's four wheeler cab in Victoria Street near the Cathedral and directed him to drive to the *Three Arrows* in Deansgate.

The two men spent about quarter of an hour in the *Three*

Arrows and on emerging instructed Henry Golding to take them to Stretford Road. Golding drove them down Peter Street and Oxford Street, and had got almost as far as Higher Cambridge Street, when he had to pull over to allow 'Mexican Joe's procession' to pass. As he started to drive again, a gentleman shouted to him that one of his cab doors was open and he had seen a young man walking away. Golding jumped down from his box and looked inside the cab. There was no sign of the younger man and the older man, who turned out to be John Fletcher, was slumped across the seats. He appeared to be drunk. Golding closed the door and got back on his box. He turned the cab round and drove straight back to where he had picked up the two men because he knew that there was a policeman on duty there and he wanted to secure his cab fare.

PC William Jakeman listened to Golding's tale, then he got into the cab and sat Fletcher upright, resting him back against the seat, raising his head as he did so. Fletcher's eyes were open but he appeared to be deeply unconscious. At first PC Jakeman thought he was simply drunk and told Golding to drive to Albert Street police station. On the way, however, PC Jakeman became increasingly concerned about Fletcher's condition and at the Parsonage near Blackfriars Bridge told the cabbie to stop. He examined Fletcher more carefully and decided that he was in fact quite seriously ill. Alarmed, Golding drove with all speed up Market Street to the Royal Infirmary in Piccadilly Gardens. As they crossed the yard of the Royal Infirmary, John Fletcher gave a deep sigh. Help had come too late. He was dead.

There were no marks of violence on the body but it appeared as though robbery could be a motive for whatever had happened to Fletcher since no money or items of any value were found on him. Initially, his sole possessions seemed to be two empty spectacle cases and a cheque book issued by the Manchester and Salford Bank; although PC Jakeman later found both pairs of spectacles inside the breast pocket of his overcoat; and there was a small gold pencil case in one of his waistcoat pockets and his shirt still had its gold studs. There was also a large bunch of keys in one of his trouser pockets. In addition there was an envelope with some indecipherable figures on it. His colleagues at the New Cannon Street offices confirmed however that when he left for lunch he had a fair sum of cash (£5 which would be worth around £330 today) in a wash-leather purse given to him that morning by one of the firm's cashiers and that he was wearing an expensive gold watch and chain together worth £120 (£7,850 at today's values).

It was established that John Fletcher had attended the mill sale at the *Mitre Hotel* for he spoke to several people there. Witnesses said they thought that he seemed to have had quite a lot to drink. However, he seemed to be in full control of himself and he bought three glasses of claret for friends and a glass of sherry for himself. When John Fletcher left the sale he announced his intention of going to Sinclair's Oyster Bar. A man named William Hall, from Saddleworth, and another man who was the brother of George Wild from Whitefield, were due to join him there, but in the end they didn't go and Mr Hall said he did not see Mr Fletcher alive again.

Edward Lait had a stall selling dried fish and game in Victoria Street adjoining Sinclairs Oyster Bar. He knew John Fletcher well and saw him that fateful Tuesday evening standing near his stall at about six-forty. He was talking to a young man and seemed the worse for drink. He was not wearing his spectacles. Edward Lait was sure on that point. PC William Jakeman had also seen John Fletcher with a young man a little further along Victoria Street near the statue of Oliver Cromwell which used to stand near Manchester Cathedral. He saw the younger man hail a cab and heard him order it to go to Deansgate. PC Jakeman managed to give a rough description of the young man: '...age about twenty two years; dressed in a dark brown suit and a pot or billycock hat, and about five feet two inches or five feet three inches in height; fresh looking; no side whiskers or moustache...'

The landlady of the *Three Arrows*, Miss Elizabeth Ross, said that the two men had come into her hotel early on the Tuesday evening. The older man had ordered two beers and she had served them in the smokeroom. In the time it took for her bring the older man his change he had drunk his beer and the two of them left soon afterwards. She thought they seemed rather quiet for they were not talking much to each other.

Barry Smith, who was employed in the shop at 43 Stretford Road where Golding had been instructed to drive after leaving the *Three Arrows*, said that he could not imagine why they were driving there. Mr Fletcher was not a customer and in any case the shop was closed at that hour and no-one lived on the premises.

One of the Coroner's jurors asked Golding why he had not just driven to All Saints police station which was nearer and Golding replied that he thought to go back the way he came. When the same juror said that it might have saved Fletcher's life if he had done so, the Coroner intervened and said that Golding hadn't realised that John Fletcher was seriously ill. Thinking him merely drunk, Golding had returned to find the policeman whom he knew had seen the two men getting into his cab.

John Fletcher was a well-known figure in Bolton and Manchester and because of this the case attracted 'a lot of excitement and attention'. The police were under pressure to make an arrest and this they did the day after the inquest, which had been held three days after Fetcher's death. Charles Parton was twenty-one-years-old and had made a name for himself as a boxer. He was arrested in the early hours as he slept at his home. Chief Detective Inspector Caminada said:

> ...I in company with two other detective officers, apprehended the prisoner at 12 Moore Street, Rochdale Road. I saw him in bed in the house, and in the room were five or six other persons. I told him that I was going to take him into custody on suspicion, that the charge was a serious one, and that he had better be very cautious how he answered the questions... and he [Parton] was identified by the cabman as being the person he drove from the Cathedral steps to the Three Arrows and to Stretford Road on Tuesday night last in company with the gentleman who is now deceased... I got a second cabman who drove him from a beerhouse in Chatham Street to Oldham Road, and he picked him out...

The problem was how had Charles Parton killed John

Fletcher? Cause of death was given as heart failure but the post-mortem had revealed Fletcher to be a healthy man, '...*internally the body was very well nourished...*', despite the fact that he was a heavy drinker, and there was nothing wrong with his heart. The pathologist stated '...*the deceased had no heart disease. Alcohol was the prevailing smell* [of the internal organs such as stomach, brain, liver]. *My examination led me to the conclusion that the deceased was a man who had led an irregular life, that he was a drunkard...*' Astonishment was expressed at this aspect of John Fletcher's character, though he had often been seen, to quote modern slang, 'well into his cups'. In Victorian England however it was neither prudent nor the 'done thing' to even suggest that a well respected and well connected member of society might have a drink problem.

It had to be some kind of poison. There really was no other conclusion. Dr John Hampden Barker had been the house physician on duty when John Fletcher was brought into the Royal Infirmary. He had examined the deceased for any unusual smell:

> ...*I examined the breath for prussic acid, applying chemical tests to the mouth, but failed to find any trace of such poison...I could say from his appearance that morphine and strychnine might be eliminated from the cause of death...*

However, Mr Charles Estcourt, the Manchester City analyst, had made an intriguing find when he analysed the intestines, stomach and stomach contents of John Fletcher. At first he could find nothing to suggest any type of 'foreign substance.' Then he carried out more detailed tests:

> ...*I examined them particularly with a view to ascertain whether or not chloroform or hydrate of chloral were present...I therefore submitted the contents to an exceedingly delicate process by which chloral hydrate is decomposed if present...the decomposition results in the production of chloroform...I did detect a trace of chloroform under such conditions which... proved that it had been derived from chloral hydrate...*

but Mr Estcourt did not consider that the trace had been sufficient to kill John Fletcher.

However, two things happened which conspired to seal Charles Parton's fate and establish his guilt. The first was the testimony of Dr Ernest Reynolds, the resident medical officer at Manchester Royal Infirmary. He suspected that death might have been caused by excess alcohol and probably the addition of chloroform, chloral, prussic acid, oxalic acid or some kind of vegetable poison. Having heard the evidence he said:

...I can safely eliminate all but alcohol and chloral...the objection to chloral is the absence of smell, which is like that of a freshly cut cucumber...but, if present, would have been overshadowed by the smell of alcohol... Alcohol, he said, would heighten the effects of choral and ...what might be a safe dose to a sober person would be dangerous under the influence of drink...

Secondly, and even more damning for Charles Parton, was that Charles Bromley, a Liverpool chemist, recognised him as the young man who had stolen a bottle of chloral hydrate from his shop one week before John Fletcher was killed. On 19 February Charles Parton had gone into his shop and asked Mr Bromley to make up a small quantity of chloral. While the chemist was doing this Parton stole a bottle containing about a pound (half a kilo) of chloral in a solid form and ran out of the shop with it. Mr Bromley identified Charles Parton without hesitation as the perpetrator of this crime.

The Coroner's jury took only a few minutes to find Charles Parton guilty of administering chloral to John Fletcher and that as this had been the cause of his death then Charles Parton was guilty of wilful murder. He was sent for trial at the City Police Court in Minshull Street. This took place early in March 1889. It was now accepted that John Fletcher had died from the effects of a combination of alcohol and chloral, and Charles Parton had been alone in the cab with him in which he was found dying and from which his purse, watch and chain had disappeared.

The police discovered that Charles, and his brother

Augustus, had been present as drinking companions on several other occasions when unsuspecting individuals suddenly found themselves in a stupor which they could not explain and when they recovered found that they had been robbed of cash and watches. These included John Parkey, a railway porter who was given drugged beer; and Samuel Oldfield, a grocer, who was also robbed in a cab and left unconscious, seemingly through drink.

Charles Parton was found guilty and sentenced to death. However there was an outcry at this decision and many letters of protest, because while it was felt that Parton had intended to rob Fletcher, he had not intended to kill him and had no idea of the *precise character and potency of chloral* which he had used to drug his victims. He could not have known that John Fletcher's state of intoxication would make the administering of chloral lethal.

A petition for reprieve was presented to the Home Secretary on the 4 April 1889. It carried 20,350 signatures including those of professional people, clergymen and merchants.

Finally, on 8 April the Home Secretary formally commuted Parton's sentence to penal servitude for life. So ended one of the strangest sagas of a 'foul deed.'

The questions remain unanswered as to why John Fletcher should choose to break his arrangement with his friend and go drinking with a young man he had never met before, and what inducements Charles Parton used to persuade Fletcher to go to an address in Stretford where he had never been before that dark February night.

CHAPTER 26

The Hanging on Bolton Moor
1786

croft breaking was... a hanging offence.

In the eighteenth century, before the days of the cotton mills, crofting was a common sight in and around Bolton. Crofting was part of the bleaching process. Cloth was soaked in lye (wood ash liquid) for a week and then soaked for a further week in a potash lye. This was known as 'bucking'. Afterwards the cloth was and put in barrels of buttermilk for another week. Finally, the cloth was spread on the grass of a bleach field, or on a frame supported by tenter posts, to dry and bleach in the sun. It was this last process which was known as crofting. While drying and bleaching in the sun the cloth was very vulnerable to theft. Stealing drying and bleaching cloth was known as croft breaking and the penalties were severe in the extreme.

James Holland was a Bolton lad in his late teens. His family was poor and there was never enough money. Crofting was a familiar sight to James. He would stand looking at the lengths of cloth slowly bleaching in the summer sunshine, wondering about the people who had enough money to buy all that cloth, thinking how much difference the sale of just one piece could make to his family. James knew the score. Croft breaking was quite literally a hanging offence. Yet one day the temptation proved too much. He stole thirty yards of cloth, costing sixty shillings (today worth £221.46) from a local bleach field belonging to Mr Thwaites's Mill in King Street, Burnden, near Bolton.

Unfortunately for James he was seen and it wasn't long before the long arm of the law had reached out to touch him with the shadow of the Grim Reaper. He was sentenced to a public execution by hanging on Bolton Moor. His family were heartbroken; pleaded that he was only a lad, but to no avail. An example had to be made and on 18 September 1786 he was hanged before a large crowd. All the employers in the neighbourhood assembled their servants and workpeople to watch James swing into eternity. His body was then suspended in a gibbet at Gallows Hill on Deane Moor near Sunning Hill★. A local watercolour artist of the day immortalised James Holland by painting a miniature of him showing the gallows standing sombrely in the background. This small picture survived and was eventually reproduced en masse, a sad and gruesome reminder of harsher times when a policy of zero tolerance meant just that.

★This grisly practice was repeated in 1797 when Samuel Longworth was gibbeted after being hanged for robbing and murdering William Horrox, aged eighteen, in Deane Church Lane, Bolton, on 27 October 1796.

James Holland's execution in 1786.
Quarry Bank Mill

CHAPTER 27

Can't Live With You,
Can't Live Without You
1857

*...He pulled a knife from his pocket
and drew it across her throat.*

Aaron Mellor was not good husband material. He didn't seem to have much trouble attracting the ladies. The problem was keeping them. By his mid-twenties he had already got through two wives. The first had died childless after two years of marriage. The fate of the second was always a matter of vagueness and conjecture. His family lived at Horton in Staffordshire but Aaron was restless. He was keen to go north and find what he hoped would be better paid work in the cotton mill towns of Lancashire where he'd heard that the streets were paved with gold and men could make a fortune.

The reality of Cottonopolis was very different as Aaron quickly discovered. The hours were long and hard; the wages were low; and there were too many men queuing for the jobs available; so he resorted to the trade he had known in Staffordshire, making and selling besoms (brooms made of wiry twigs tied to a long central handle, like the popular image of witch's broomsticks). He settled in Bolton and made a poor kind of itinerant living. Aaron was personable enough: '...a thin spare man of ruddy countenance and sandy hair, and stands about five feet six inches in height...'; but he had a weakness for drink and when he was drunk he was violent. He kept bad company and was not generally considered by the mothers of Bolton to be much of a catch for their daughters.

Alice Mulloy didn't care. She was an attractive girl, rather small in height, but she had a good figure, a dark complexion and black hair. Alice met Aaron in 1850 when she was sixteen and, much to her mother's horror, moved in with him when she was seventeen. She was soon pregnant, confirming her mother's worst fears, but Aaron did the decent thing and married her in 1852. They had little money and home was a poorly furnished cellar on Velvet Walks in Bolton. Aaron continued to make and sell besoms; and in winter, when the ling for the besoms was difficult to obtain, he sold pots. Alice took in washing and also went out to do washing. She was regarded as much the more industrious one of the pair.

On 9 January 1857 Alice celebrated her twenty third birthday. She had been married to Aaron for five years and she'd already had four children. Their eldest child, and the reason for their marriage, had recently died. The remaining children were a girl of four and two boys, one aged three, the other about six months old. It was an unhappy marriage. Aaron was now thirty three and drinking a lot. There were violent quarrels and he often beat Alice, leaving her a mass of black and blue bruises. He frequently failed to provide for her and the children and she usually had a rather starved appearance. Finally Alice had had enough and on Saturday, 26 September 1857 she left him.

Alice left the two older children with John Garratts and his family who lived on Velvet Walks in the neighbouring cellar,

Left: *The* Old Three Crowns *on the corner of Deansgate and Crown Street near which Alice and Aaron had their last argument.*

Below: *Crown Street today, where Alice Mellor was murdered.* The author

while she took the baby and returned to her mother's home. Ann Mulloy was a widow and she had a small house on Back Crown Street. Alice spent her days there with her mother but she slept at the house of Dan Cunningham, a family friend, who lived in Smithy Street Little Bolton. Her mother, who had never liked Aaron, was not surprised by this turn of events, and told Alice that she would do what she could to help.

The following Thursday, around noon, Aaron and his neighbour, John Garratts, went into Halliwell, drinking as usual, and ended up at *Kirkman's Beer House* on New Road. It was there that Garratts noticed a knife in Aaron's breast pocket. Aaron showed it to him and claimed the knife had been lost for a few days and that he'd just found it again. They returned to Bolton and parted company in Higher Bridge Street at about seven o'clock in the evening. Aaron went straight to his mother-in-law's house and begged to speak to Alice. He asked her if she would come home but she retorted that she had no home, that the cellar was cold and that there was no fire lit. They argued for a while then, seeing it was useless to try and get her to change her mind, Aaron agreed that they should separate and he proposed that he should take one child, she the other two. Alice agreed to this and Aaron left.

Alice ate a little supper and then set off for the Cunningham's house accompanied by her mother. Near the

Bradshawgate (looking south) from the corner of Deansgate. It still retains its Victorian aspect. The author

bridge in Crown Street Aaron came running after them. They stopped for him to catch up and Alice's mother told him that they were going to a baker's near *The Roebuck* to get some bread for the children's supper. Aaron didn't believe this and said that the children didn't need any bread for their supper. Alice's mother rounded on Aaron angrily and accused him of drinking all day, not caring about his family. Of course the children wanted their supper. All three continued along Crown Street, arguing furiously. Yet again Aaron begged Alice to return to him and this time she agreed.

No one knows why Alice agreed to go back to Aaron. Perhaps she felt it was her duty; perhaps she was trying to shield her mother; perhaps she just wanted less hassle. Aaron turned to his mother-in-law and told her to go home as he was not married to her to which she retorted 'No! But you're married to my child!' He then threatened her and told her to go home or else.... Ann Mulloy reluctantly crossed the street and watched while Alice and Aaron walked slowly across Deansgate together, Alice still holding her baby. A few moments later she heard a scream.....

Alice and Aaron had begun to quarrel again as they walked along Crown Street. William Hampson, a porter who worked at Scowcroft's druggist's shop on the corner of Crown Street, had seen Mrs Mulloy leave them and he saw Alice and Aaron arguing. As they reached the top of Crown Street, Aaron pushed Alice. Opposite Scowcrofts he got hold of Alice by the shoulder but she pushed him away. Aaron caught his foot in an iron ring in the channel of the footpath used to lower goods into Scowcroft's cellar and almost fell over. He threatened to hit Alice. She asked for money to buy food but he wanted to go into *Blake's Vaults* in the Old Shambles to continue his drinking. The quarrelling escalated and Aaron punched Alice in the face. She fell and Aaron caught her and, throwing his left arm around her neck, he pulled the knife from his pocket and drew it across her throat.

Alice screamed, 'a fear inspiring, ear piercing scream' which was heard from Bradshawgate corner to Deansgate according to one witness, and fell to the ground, dropping her baby as she did so. Aaron dropped beside her on one knee and with the knife began to 'saw away at her neck...' She screamed and screamed; the most dreadful blood choked sounds. People passing by screamed as well. One of them, Edward Duckworth, a young cabinet maker, rushed at Aaron, seized his collar and dragged him forcibly off Alice. Once on his feet Aaron turned quickly and drew the knife across his own throat. He succeeded in severing his jugular vein and his windpipe before collapsing in a pool of blood.

PC George Sharples, who was near the *Rope and Anchor Inn*, rushed to the scene. He called for a doctor who examined Alice and then ordered her to be taken to the Infirmary at once. Mr Hamer of the *Red Lion* identified Aaron as Alice's attacker before he too was taken to the Infirmary. Alice was carried, blood streaming from her wounds, down Deansgate, Bradshawgate, Fold Street and Bowkers Row. Here they were met by Sergeant James Grimes and it was here that Alice died. She had bled to death. Aaron was carried to the Infirmary by a shorter route through the Shambles, Shipgates, along Mealhouse Lane and Bowkers Row and actually arrived at the Infirmary before Alice.

Although close to death, Aaron's life was saved by the quick thinking of Dr Livy, Dr Seger and Mr Ferguson; but for poor Alice it was all too late. Aaron was admitted to the hospital and placed under police guard. When he learned that Alice was

Alice pushed him and turned away, still holding her baby. Hannah Niblett

dead he appeared absolutely distraught and admitted what he had done; although he blamed his mother-in-law and her nagging about money. Beside himself with his grief, he tried to re-injure his throat; he wanted to hang himself; he wanted to drown himself in the canal; he wanted the police officers to beat his brains out with their truncheons. Ironically, having done so much to save him, the State was soon to grant his wish. At the Inquest, which was held at two o'clock on Saturday, 3 October, the Coroner's Jury returned a verdict of wilful murder against him and he was committed to trial at the Crown Court where he was found guilty of murder and sentenced to death.

Did Aaron really love Alice and did she love him? Maybe. Some couples thrive on conflict although it did seem as though Alice had finally tired of his ways. He may have loved her but he didn't treat her well. She had a cold pitiful comfortless cellar in which to live and she couldn't afford to feed her children properly. When she died all that was found in her pockets were three half pennies and two pawn tickets. Had he meant to kill her? His seeming show of remorse might indicate not, but why had he taken the knife with him that fateful day? He was used to handing out threats and violence but perhaps he had only intended to frighten her so that she would come back to him. If he had just found it again, as he said he had, he could have left in his cellar home when he called for his neighbour, John Garratts, to go drinking with him. It begins to seem that he did have a motive for having the knife in his pocket although he may not have actually intended to kill Alice. Whatever his real reason was for having the knife with him, he took that reason to his grave.

After the deaths of Aaron and Alice their families seemed unable or unwilling to take in their three children and the little ones were taken to Bolton Workhouse. Here they would have been brought up, unloved and unwanted, until at the age of eight or nine they would have been apprenticed to the local cotton mills to work for a few pence a week until they were twenty-one. It was a double tragedy: the death of the parents followed by the tragic waste of their children's lives.

CHAPTER 28

Death Stalked the Tight Rope
1859

The show had to go on.

When Pablo Fanque's circus arrived in Bolton in the spring of 1859 there was great excitement in the town. A girl billed as 'a female Blondin' was going to attempt a walk across a rope stretched taut from the third floor of the old Coronation Mills to the top of the circus tent, some sixty feet above ground level. She would walk a distance of about eighty feet to the circus tent and then retrace her steps back to the Mills. There would be no safety net and her life would be reliant upon her own skills and concentration. Someone, however, did not want this girl's walk to be successful. Someone with a grudge maybe or someone who was just jealous.

Blondin was a French tight rope walker renowned for his daring feats on the tight rope and his success in twice crossing Niagara Falls on a tight rope. He had appeared at the Crystal Palace several times in 1862 before embarking on a performance tour of England and his exploits were well known and much talked about. It was therefore with pleasurable anticipation that a crowd gathered on a night in early May to watch this 'female Blondin strut her stuff.'

She did not appear to be nervous. She scrambled out of a third floor window of the Coronation Mills and stood on the windowsill, steadying herself, trim and erect in her bright costume. Someone handed her the light pole she would use to help her balance and at seven thirty she started to carefully edge her way across the

A crowd gathered to watch this 'female Blondin strut her stuff.' Hannah Niblett

rope. To her horror however, there was a thick knot tied in the rope some fifteen feet distant from the start. Who had done this? Could they not know how dangerous it was? She tried to cross it but failed and turned, making her way a little unsteadily back to the safety of the windowsill.

While she regained her breath she considered what to do. Someone, she thought, did not want her to do this walk, and that only strengthened her determination. So much depended upon it. Her reputation and that of the circus. How could she hold her head up if she backed out now. She would not be robbed of this opportunity to display her skills and enjoy her triumph and her audience must not be disappointed. The show had to go on.

Gingerly she began her walk again. At least this time she was aware of the obstacle which lay in her path. She approached the knot slowly, gracefully lifting her front foot over it and then her back foot. She so very nearly made it but the tip of her back foot just caught the knot and she stumbled. There was a gasp of horror from the waiting crowd. She threw aside the pole and, grasping the rope with hands, she hung here suspended sixty feet above the ground.

'Lower the rope! Lower the rope!' someone shouted. The rope was lowered but it was only possible to lower it a few feet. Her arms were aching. She could not hold on much long. On the ground far below her there was some quick thinking and a group of young men massed themselves underneath where she clung desperately to the rope. 'Jump!' they yelled up to her. 'We will catch you!' She looked down at them and, then, after a moment's hesitation she let go of the rope.

Miraculously, she was caught. She wasn't even injured but she was very shaken. The police were called for it was quite obvious that the rope had been deliberately knotted and that whoever had done it intended her to fall, and it was a fall which would almost certainly have killed her. The culprit was never caught but the case was curious enough to merit an article in the *Illustrated Police News* on 15 May 1869. It is not recorded what became of the 'female Blondin' who had risked everything for her moment of glory, but it is to be hoped that, like her namesake, she lived to a good age and died safely in her bed.

CHAPTER 29

A Luddite Tragedy
1812

*...he was still screaming as the trap door opened
and swung him to darkness.*

The new mechanisation of the Industrial Revolution meant that spinning and weaving of cloth could be done far more quickly and efficiently than ever before. This hit the hand-loom weavers particularly hard. By 1812 the war, taxes and the depression of trade (caused by the British fight against Napoleon and his allies) and the high price of corn and other provisions had brought them to their knees. Whole families went for days without food. Children pleaded, mothers cried, fathers were desperate. Tensions and resentments simmered. Something had to give.

Men began banding together into groups to try and do something about the situation. Around November 1811 a 'brotherhood' was formed in the neighbourhood of Chowbent, close to Bolton. Secret meetings took place around midnight in isolated places up on the nearby moors. They had to be careful. If even a word of their activities reached the ears of the authorities they were in big trouble. Officialdom was very tetchy these days; a result no doubt of the recent French Revolution. There the workers, the ordinary people, had shown in no uncertain terms that they were a force to be reckoned with, and that when they were treated with contempt they were prepared to do something about it, with violence if need be.

On 20 March 1812 a meeting of the 'new brotherhood, bound by oath, with the object of revolutionising the country...' (known as Luddites who believed that if they smashed up the new machinery the old way of life would return) took place at Clapperfold on Deane Moor and it was proposed that the Wroe and Duncough cotton mill at Westhoughton just outside Bolton should be 'torched'. On 19 April a group set out to march to Westhoughton with that objective in mind. This would an open show of their strength and purpose and they needed support. They had passed a resolution to 'twist or puff' (swear or shoot) everyone they met on their way. Not wanting to be shot on the spot, people swore their oath and the new movement prided itself on its swelling numbers.

News of their arrival and intentions preceded them. The 'brotherhood' reached Westhoughton on 24 April and gathered in the market place there where they were joined by more local people. Then they marched four deep to the factory. Forcing an entrance they smashed the wooden looms and wrapped the cloth around the beams. An eyewitness recounts what happened next:

> *...the mill, a few moments earlier a model of cleanliness and neatness, was strewn with the fragments like swathes of grass...John Seddon then said "the egg is broken; let us burn the shell." A shovelful of fire was placed in a calico "cut", laid down on the floor, and the broken looms piled around it. A hogshead of tallow was rolled into the fire. A number of women danced a reel around the blazing heap. Then the cry was raised "every man to his tent O Israel!" and each tried to get home unobserved...*

However, forces of law and order had arrived from Bolton.

'the egg is broken; let us burn the shell.' Hannah Niblett

Magistrates read the Riot Act to the crowd outside and sent in the Scots Greys to deal with the disturbance. About a dozen people were arrested. They were tried at Lancaster castle on 1 June. The trial began at seven in the morning and lasted until eleven at night. Job Fletcher, James Smith, Thomas Kerfoot and Abraham Charleston of Westhoughton were found guilty while eight others were acquitted. The Manchester and Middleton rioters were then tried while the Westhoughton men speculated as to the sentences they would receive which they thought would probably be brief varying terms of imprisonment; but the court was determined to make a stand.

A writer covering the trial describes what happened:

> *...I believe it never entered the mind of any of them that they would get more than three to six month's imprisonment. They were called upon to receive their sentences, and I shall never forget the look of horror on the face of Job Fletcher. I was getting some dinner ready for him when he went, and he came back in a few minutes, and grasped me by the collar in a phrenzied manner "O dear, dear!" cried he, "I'm to be hanged!" Others came in who had received the same sentence, and the most heart-rendering scene took place that it is possible for the mind to conceive. Some threw themselves on the floor, others tore hair from their heads, bitterly cursing the witnesses who had appeared against them, and lamenting that they must never more see their families. They were taken from us to the condemned cells, and I never saw any more of them...*

The executions took place shortly afterwards on 11 June. Job Fletcher, James Smith and Thomas Kerfoot tried to maintain some semblance of manly dignity on the scaffold, but Abraham Charleton was a boy of just twelve and he was absolutely terrified. He screamed 'Oh mammy! mammy!' as the noose was put round his neck, and he was still screaming as the trap door opened and swung him into the darkness.

However, it appeared that the authorities might have been every bit as culpable in this tragedy as the 'brotherhood.' It seemed as though they had got wind of what was to happen and planned in advance to 'allow' it so that a violent example could be made of the perpetrators which they hoped would deter others from similar action. Before the fire the mill had been guarded round the clock for many weeks by constables from Bolton. For 'some inexplicable reason' as a contemporary writer noted, they were withdrawn the day and night before the fire occurred. Before the fire soldiers also went to Westhoughton daily, riding out from Bolton sometimes twice a day, some times three times. In a corner of the mill fifty loaded muskets had been piled up and these exploded during the course of the fire.

The whole episode left a nasty taste in the mouths of many Boltonians. It was made a great deal worse by the suspicion and then the discovery that the Bolton magistrates had planted spies and agitators among the rioters. Several had attended the meeting on the night of 19 April at Deane Moor, armed and disguised with blackened faces. They were reputed to be in the employ of a Colonel Fletcher. During the disturbances they wore white caps so that the military would recognise them and not molest them.

The 'black-faced spies' continued their work even after these events because the end of the Napoleonic Wars did not herald a return to prosperity and there was still great agitation for reform. The French Revolution still fresh in their minds, the authorities were not taking any chances. If 'agent provocateurs' (dissenters encouraging the use of violence) could provoke a little civil disorder here and there it would give the authorities the excuse they needed for harsh and draconian measures against those who tried to refuse to put up with high prices and low wages or unemployment.

One of the most notorious and hated of these 'blackfaced spies' was a Bolton man named Waddington. In 1818 he incited a number of riots in the town, being always careful to remain in the background. One day, in that same year, he was walking through Bolton when he was recognised by a young school teacher who openly denounced him. Waddington's response was to produce a gun and shoot the school teacher in the thigh. He was arrested, bailed and quietly disappeared; while the hapless school teacher found himself nursing a gunshot wound and, to rub salt into this wound, he was 'indicted and convicted for riot at Salford Assizes.'

CHAPTER 30

Blood Feud
1851

...wooden clogs were a lethal weapon.

D runken brawls were common enough in nineteenth century Bolton. When under the influence of too much beer or too much gin, men and women perceived slights where none was intended or some minor matter was blown up out of all proportion. Scuffles broke out and frequently erupted into the street. Often a small crowd would gather, cheering and egging the others on. Finally, when someone's nose had been bloodied or someone's eye had been blackened, they would all go back into the pub and have yet another drink. What made this case different was a sudden escalation of the violence by the crowd who seemed to adopt a mob mentality and attacked one of the fighters for not being violent enough with the result that a man was kicked to death by his own brother.

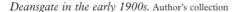

Deansgate in the early 1900s. Author's collection

Thomas Murray, a twenty-six-year-old labourer, and his wife, Catherine, lived near the *Wellington* public house on Gartside Street off Deansgate in Bolton. It was Saturday night and they were going out for an evening of drinking and dog fighting at the pub. It was a good night and they enjoyed themselves. Just after ten thirty Thomas Murray left the pub for a few minutes. While he was gone, Catherine got into some argument with William Ball, a collier who lived round the corner on Sidney Street. The quarrel escalated rapidly with William and Catherine shouting at each other and she calling him a bully. His response was to slap her round the face hard.

At this point Thomas returned and, outraged that Ball had hit his wife, challenged him to a fight. They fought in the street for about six or seven minutes. Murray swiftly got the upper hand, loudly encouraged by Catherine. A crowed of friends and associates had gathered and were cheering the two men on. Both men were on the ground, but although Ball was underneath and Murray had the upper hand, he did little to hurt Ball. Some of the crowd started to denounce Thomas as 'soft' and, spoiling for more of a show, began kicking him. One of those kicking Thomas was his own brother, Hugh Murray, an eighteen year old moulder. Another was Thomas Lord, a collier who had been drinking with Ball. Yet another man, named Patrick Regan joined in. The kicking became more violent and Hugh Murray aimed some vicious kicks at his brother's body with his hobnailed clogs.

Suddenly, Thomas collapsed. By this time the police had been called and everyone was arrested, including an innocent passer-by named Patrick Regan. Thomas was taken home and put to bed. He did not recover however. Two days later, on Monday, 30 May 1851, he died as a result of a rupture under the right lobe of his liver. At the inquest every one was cleared and released however except Hugh Murray, the brother of the dead man. The Coroner's jury decided that the violence of Hugh Murray's kicks justified indicting him on a charge of manslaughter, and the Coroner remarked sombrely it was high time that it was recognised that wooden clogs were a lethal weapon and were employed far too often as such.

CHAPTER **31**

Death of a Farmer
1856

He was hurting and held his hand over his bowels.

On Monday, 22 December 1856 an inquest was held at the *Victory Inn* in Halliwell to determine exactly who or what killed John Dugdale, a forty-seven-year-old farmer of Shipton's Halliwell near Bolton. The victim died at four o'clock in the afternoon on the 18 December at his home, clear in his own mind as to the cause of his death; but, as the Coroner's jury discovered, the case was not quite that straightforward. It was, in fact, rather complicated, and the story is best told through the witnesses at the inquest as the jury would have heard it.

Mary Dugdale, also aged forty-seven years, had been married to John for about twenty-five years. She said that he had come home late after going out drinking on the night of Friday, 12 December. His trousers were torn and dirty. He said that he had been involved in a fight with Rhodes's sons. They had lugged him and throttled him and he thought they would rob him; but he made no complaint about being in any pain and went to bed. Next morning he was up at seven-thirty to take the milk from their cows into Bolton. He 'never complained more about the Rhodes sons except to say he should have taken out a warrant'.

The following Tuesday afternoon he came in from the barn to say he'd slipped one leg through a hole in the balks and hurt his shin bone. He made 'no complaints about feeling poorly and went about his business and with the milk up to Wednesday night'. He took the milk to Bolton on the Wednesday evening but not on the following morning. On the Thursday morning at around five o'clock he had complained of 'gripe in his belly'. He got up at nine and went downstairs, but returned with his clothes in his hand and said that he 'was done for; he would never mend.' He was hurting and held his hand over his bowels. He went back to bed but got up a little later to have a bath, then returned to his bed. The following afternoon at about four-thirty he died.

Thomas Henry Dugdale, John Dugdale's son was cutting hay in the barn for the cattle that Tuesday afternoon when he his father's leg slipped through a foot square hole in the balks. His father swore, but he 'didn't fall on his belly'. Thomas remembered his father telling him that he had been beaten up by the Rhodes sons.

John Dugdale's brother-in-law, Jabez Parker, who farmed at Tonge-with-Haulgh near Bolton, said that Dugdale knew he was going to die and that the Rhodes sons had killed him. John had told him that the previous Friday night he and three of the Rhodes sons had been drinking in Bolton. As they were walking home up the road John had asked them for repayment of a half crown which he'd lent them some time before. Things had then become unpleasant and they had started throttling him and kicking him. He called for help and a man named James Wignall had come to his aid. John said that he'd been feeling sore because they had kicked him in the belly; but he'd not dared to get a warrant because they were dangerous young men.

James Wignall, a watchman at Cannon and Haslam's mill, confirmed Jabez' story. He had seen John Dugdale and the taller of the Rhodes sons (the one who was married) pass by the factory gates at around one o'clock in the morning. A short while he later he heard cries and hurried out. He had found John with the three Rhodes sons and their mother. The taller lad had his hands round John's neck and one of the younger unmarried sons was kicking him in the belly. John seemed to be walking lame. Mrs Rhodes told Wignall to go away (this was witnessed by a man named John Parker). All the Rhodes boys seemed to be drunk, a fact corroborated by William Wightman, landlord of the *Victory Tavern*.

The medical evidence did little to make the situation clearer. Dr Livy, who attended John Dugdale, said that John had had a fall from a hayloft and that he'd also complained of abdominal pain. The post-mortem had revealed finger and thumb marks on either side of the throat. The abdomen, intestines and bowel were full of blood from a ruptured blood vessel and this had been the cause of death. External violence had been the cause of the rupture but John had not complained of 'any abuse.' Dr Livy said that the rupture had 'been effected some thirty hours before death' but the injury which caused the rupture could have 'been effected some days before death.' The doctor thought that the injury may have been received through 'a crush with a knee rather than a kick with a clog' because there were no external marks. He felt that John Dugdale might have recovered from the initial beating given to him by the Rhodes boys if he'd taken care of himself; but he had gone straight back to work instead.

Peter Dobson of *St George's Tavern*, Little Bolton, did his best to cloud the issue and told a story of John Dugdale falling down some steps when he left the tavern by the back door instead of going out of the front door with his son. He'd given John some brandy while his son was looking for him,

The Hen & Chickens *public house on Deansgate where John Dugdale watched a shooting match.* Author's collection

wondering what had become of him. However, John Dugdale's son denied this and there were no marks on Dugdale's body to suggest that he'd fallen down any steps.

The Coroner ordered the Rhodes sons to be arraigned. John Rhodes, aged thirty-one, a stonemason, and his brother, William, aged twenty-nine, also a stonemason, were indicted for the manslaughter of John Dugdale.

When they appeared in court yet another version of events was given. John Dugdale had gone to *St George's Tavern*, telling his son he would meet him there later. Dugdale had left the *Tavern* to go to the *Hen and Chickens* to watch a shooting match. When he returned to *St George's* he met up with John and William Rhodes. They had drunk rum punch together until midnight. Dugdale's son was tired and went home early,

The Alma Inn, *a surviving Victorian public house on Bradshawgate.*
Author's collection

leaving his father with the Rhodes lads. It was about an hour later that the fracas took place. James Wignall saw John Rhodes holding Dugdale against the wall by the shoulder with his left hand, trying to throttle him with his right hand, while William was kicking him in the belly. Wignall had separated them and stayed with Dugdale until a couple of neighbours took him home around two in the morning.

Mr Monk, for the defence, contended however that because there were no external marks on John Dugdale and he continued to work after the fight, then the fall could just as easily have killed him. He might have suffered an internal injury which would have healed naturally had he not then had his accident in the barn. The jury took just twenty minutes to find John and William Rhodes not guilty and they were acquitted.

CHAPTER 32

A Death Waiting to Happen
1902

Mrs Hague heard piercing screams...

Even by the brutal standards that were acceptable in the nineteenth century for beating wives and girlfriends this case is extraordinary not only for the exceptional amount of violence used over a very short period, but also for the acceptance and apparent understanding shown by the victim. To modern ways of thinking it is inexplicable that when even when she had nothing more to lose the girl on whom the violence was inflicted without mercy, causing her agonised suffering, still did her utmost to protect the wretched man who had treated her in such an inhuman way. Curiously enough, they both protested that he 'only did it because he loved her'; that he was 'being cruel to be kind.'

Henry Mack was born Henry McWiggin in Bolton in 1873. He was a bright and intelligent lad who could have had a prosperous future but he got in with a bad lot at school and began to play truant. It is a depressingly familiar story. Instead of working hard and building a decent career for himself he began hawking with a donkey and cart and when that did not bring as much money as he wanted he turned to a life of crime. He committed his offence in 1885 when he was just twelve, stealing a jersey for which he was given nine strokes of the birch. It had little effect on him. By 1888 he was serving his first prison term, this time for stealing pies. The police blamed his environment. His parents, though respectable enough, were very poor, living in one of the more disreputable parts of Bolton, where Henry mixed with undesirable companions. When and why Henry changed his surname isn't known, but it is probable that he adopted his nickname of 'Mack' when he was on the run to try and avoid detection.

After he was released from prison his crimes began to

escalate. He robbed a local shop till and went to Blackpool where he committed more robberies, some of them with violence if the unfortunate owners showed reluctance to part with their goods or cash. By now the police were hot on his trail and Henry decided that it would be prudent to make himself scarce so he went to the Isle of Man to escape the long arm of the law. His luck had run out however. A Bolton policeman who was on holiday in the Isle of Man saw Henry Mack and recognised him. Henry was duly arrested and returned to Bolton where he was sentenced to a further term of imprisonment.

Leopards don't change their spots and Henry Mack proved no exception to this rule. As soon as he was free he resumed his life of crime; although his occupation was officially stated as that of a 'labourer'. He was usually caught and he was sent to prison on several occasions. When he committed a highway robbery with violence he was given twenty lashes with the 'cat' (a leather whip with nine thongs) which must have really hurt, but nothing would deter him from his chosen life of crime. Eventually Bolton became 'too hot' for him and he absconded to Oldham, a town a few miles distant.

Esther Elizabeth Bradford was also known to the Bolton police. She was born in Mechanic Street off Folds Road in Bolton and continued living there with her mother when she reached adulthood. Esther got a job in the card room of a local mill and worked there diligently enough until she met Barney Dunn. Barney had a reputation as a 'drunken hooligan', as the police termed him, but he could be charming enough when he wanted to be and it did not take him long to get Esther under his spell. She left her mother's home and moved in with Barney. They went drinking together and it wasn't long before Esther was sent to prison for drunk and disorderly behaviour.

Esther continued to live with Barney Dunn until June 1902 when she met Henry Mack. The circumstances of their meeting are unknown. Perhaps Henry had sneaked a rare visit home to see his family. It must have been a case of love at first sight or, at the very least, an instant attraction, because Esther left Barney almost immediately and went to live with Mack in the room of a house at Hopwood in Oldham. This did not please Barney too much but he knew of Mack's reputation and decided to let well alone. As far as he was concerned they were welcome to each other and good riddance.

It was obvious to Esther that she had a problem with her drinking but it was the only way she knew of relieving the despondency she felt about her life. She seemed to have lost the hope that things would improve; lost sight of the light at the end of the tunnel. Every time she went on a bender she promised herself it would be the last. Until the next time. Barney hadn't seemed to mind her drinking. In fact he'd encouraged her at times. He'd been rather more laid back than Mack. She loved Mack desperately but she sensed things simmering in him that she didn't understand.

Esther and Mack seemed to have lived happily enough together for a few weeks, however, but trouble was brewing. On 2 August Mack was seen dragging Esther about in the street, kicking her and beating her. A neighbour tried to intervene and persuade him to stop but Mack dragged Esther back into their room and locked the door. Esther, frantic to escape him, opened the window and jumped about twelve feet to the ground. She sustained some cuts and bruising, and she was a bit shocked, but she seemed to be otherwise unhurt.

A week later, on 8 August, Esther annoyed him again by cooking only a plate of potatoes for his dinner. She probably had no money to buy and cook anything more but this would have been of little account to Mack. He took the plate of potatoes to a neighbour, Mrs Hague, and asked if she thought that was a good enough dinner for him, then he stormed back to his room, kicked Esther hard and punched her, giving her two black eyes. The next day they quarrelled all day. Mack asked the neighbours in the adjoining room if Esther had been drinking but they said that she hadn't. Mack did not believe them. He beat Esther up again and struck her in the face with a shovel. The neighbours offered to call the police but Esther refused. Mack then gave her a good kicking, continuing to kick her mercilessly until she was bleeding at the nose and mouth.

Unbelievably, despite this dreadful treatment, Esther went out to the pub with him that night as though nothing had happened. Maybe she was too scared to refuse and desperate to humour him at all costs. Maybe, and more than likely, she needed a stiff drink. However by eleven o'clock he told her to go home as she was the worse for drink but Esther refused and was given another good kicking.

The following day, 10 August, Esther and Mack were peaceable together. Esther, hurting from her beatings, and probably suffering from a hangover, lay in bed and tried to rest. She did not go out that night, but the next day around three in the afternoon, their neighbour, Mrs Hague, heard piercing screams coming from Mack and Esther's room. Mrs Hague rushed in to find that Esther had been badly scalded on her face. Esther said that she'd scalded herself but Mrs Hague noted the kettle at the foot of the bed while its lid lay on the pillow and water ran down the walls. Mack was running away from the house. Mrs Hague heard Mack return and went out across the landing to the doorway of their room. Esther asked Mack for some brandy because she was feeling really ill. Mack stared at her with contempt.

'You cow!' he spat and smacked her across her scalded face which burst one of the blisters. Esther screamed in agony and pleaded with him.

'Oh Mack don't! You will kill me!'

'That,' he replied, 'is exactly what I intend to do!'

Mack went out and Mrs Hague sat with the distressed and hurting girl. Esther was too poor to call a doctor, too frightened to call the police. She could only lie there and wait. Around eleven thirty five Mack returned with another man and ordered Mrs Hague to go home. At midnight he began to assault Esther again. He dragged her off the bed, kicking her lower body, then, holding her legs, dashed her against the wall of the room. Mrs Hague heard her crying ' Oh my! Oh my!' Esther lay on the floor sobbing but Mack picked her up and threw her back on the bed and then began to jump up and down on her as she lay prostrate. Mrs Hague could stand no more. She rushed back into the room and asked if she should go for a doctor. Mack whirled round and snarled at her

'If you do that I shall stick a fork in your heart!'

Mrs Hague fled back to her room.

The next morning, however, Mack went for the doctor; the

same doctor to whom he had complained previously about Esther's drinking habits. She had a fondness for rum and stout. The doctor examined Esther. She had suffered severe internal injuries and her face was a mess. She was taken to the Infirmary where she died the following day. Esther knew she was dying and she gave a statement to the police but she refused to blame Mack. Instead she tried to shield him by saying that she had scalded herself and that she had deserved the beatings which had only occurred when she was drunk. It is hard to understand her reasons for protecting Mack. She knew she was dying and so had nothing left to fear from him. She may have really loved him, and believed that he loved her, but in the three months they had been together he had shown her little kindness and a great deal of vicious cruelty.

Mack's cruelty to Esther shocked even those who accepted that a man had a right to beat his wife. He was committed for trial on a charge of wilful murder. Despite his grievous ill treatment of Esther, the defence lawyer, Mr Jordan, asked for a charge of manslaughter, based on Esther's statement. The judge refused absolutely and directed that the jury should bring in a verdict of murder or nothing. This time Mack had gone too far; much too far. He was found guilty of wilful murder. Asked if he had anything to say why the sentence of death should not be passed on him, Mack replied:

My Lord, no-one on this earth thought more of that woman than I did. In fact, when I had known her to be drunk I left my business as a bookmaker, where I earned £2 and £3 a week, found her, and brought her home.

The judge was unimpressed and donned his black cap. As he sentenced Mack to death by hanging at Strangeways Prison on 9 December 1902 the judge remarked that 'this person will pass into the Great Beyond unwept, unhonoured and unsung.'

Acknowledgements

Grateful thanks are due to the staff at Bolton Local Studies Library, to my long suffering family and to Wharncliffe Books for the help and guidance they have given me during the researching and writing of *Foul Deeds and Suspicious Deaths* during 400 years of Bolton's history.

Index